VENICE

DEDICATION

To Betty & Eddie, Hilary & Frank

V E N I C E

AN ARCHITECTURAL GUIDE / EDWINA BIUCCHI AND SIMON PILLING
PHOTOGRAPHS BY KEITH COLLIE

BATSFORD

BRITISH LIBRARY CATALOGUING IN PUBLICATION
A CIP RECORD FOR THIS BOOK IS AVAILABLE FROM THE BRITISH LIBRARY

PUBLISHED BY B T BATSFORD
64 BREWERY ROAD, LONDON N7 9NT
WWW.BATSFORD.COM
SERIES EDITOR TOM NEVILLE
SERIES DESIGN CLAUDIA SCHENK

FIRST PUBLISHED 2002
COPYRIGHT © 2002 B T BATSFORD, A member of Chrysalis Books plc

ISBN 0 7134 8781 X

PRINTED IN SPAIN BY JUST COLOUR GRAPHIC, S.L.

FOR A COPY OF THE BATSFORD CATALOGUE OR INFORMATION
ON SPECIAL QUANTITY ORDERS OF BATSFORD BOOKS PLEASE
CONTACT US ON 020 7697 3000 OR SALES@CHRYSALISBOOKS.CO.UK

Simon Pilling and Edwina Biucchi 2002

CONTENTS

INTRODUCTION

It's July 1574, and the Venetian Republic – La Serenissima – is in final preparation for the state visit of King Henri III of France. The approach to the city, almost 300 years before any land bridge connection, comes from the Adriatic through the narrow channels of the Lido, where a temporary triumphal arch, designed by Palladio and decorated by Tintoretto and Veronese, has been erected. The king is to cross the Lagoon on a ship powered by 400 Slav oarsmen, alongside which a floating furnace – constructed in the form of a fiery sea monster – creates glass trinkets for his amusement. His short stay in Venice, in the sumptuous Ca' Foscari on the Grand Canal, will be marked by the ostentatious bravado for which the city was infamous and which, it is suggested, left the young king in a state of bemusement for life.

When faced with today's tourism-dominated city it is hard to comprehend the influence that this city-state once exerted across the medieval and renaissance world. Today it is its architecture – the tangible demonstration of individual and state wealth – that most powerfully testifies to Venice's extraordinary history.

Origins

Venetia – the mainland coastal area which surrounds the Lagoon – was settled by the Romans in the 1st century BC, its administrative centre the city of Aquileia. When, in 330, the empire's capital was moved to Constantinople the region became a province of this eastern empire – Byzantium – thus establishing the link that would ultimately lead to Venice's position at the fulcrum of eastern and western civilisations. The connection with Byzantium was not just political but also religious in that the Venetian church looked to the Eastern Roman Emperor, not the Pope, for guidance; this was to increasingly become a source of friction between Venice and the church of Rome.

The Venetian Lagoon has been inhabited since the 5th century, when its numerous small islands first became a temporary refuge for people from the mainland avoiding the repeated northern European attacks on the disintegrating Western Roman Empire. A swampland with an average depth of water of one metre, the Lagoon, formed at the estuary of the Brenta and Sile rivers, is protected from the Adriatic sea by a string of narrow landstrips know as Lidi (today consolidated as Pellestrina, Lido and Cavallino). Having gradually established communities on the Lagoon, the inhabitants increasingly sought independence from the mainland. By the end of the 7th century they had elected their first Doge and in 810 moved the future Republic's seat of power from Malamocco on the Lido to the Lagoon's central islands – the Rivo Alto (later abbreviated to Rialto when naming Venice's central commercial district) – building on the site still used by today's Palazzo Ducale.

The winged lion of Venice

Seen throughout Venice, adorning many of its buildings, the winged lion is the symbol of the Republic. The remains of St Mark were stolen from Alexandria and brought to Venice in 829 – considered morally defensible because St Mark had supposedly travelled to Roman Aquileia on the adjacent mainland in AD 42 and established a Christian church. The history was further embellished by the assertion that, while stranded in the Venetian Lagoon, St Mark had heard the message – *Pax Tibi Marce, Evangelista Meus. Hic requiescat corpus tuum.* (Peace to you, Mark, my Evangelist. This will be your resting place.) Hence, the winged lion holds the book, open at this text, which Venice adopted as a direct message to the Republic to justify its imperial ambitions.

Architecture and trade

Venetian architecture is a unique response to a unique situation, accommodating a society both physically and politically based on water. With no natural resources of its own, Venice's existence was, from the outset, reliant on trade. So successful was it to prove in this that by the late 15th century the Venetian Republic had effectively taken control of all major trade between Europe and the East, having finally seen off its major Italian rivals – Genoa and Pisa. Venice was then at the height of its power – a cosmopolitan city dedicated to the facilitation of trade and symbolically and geographically at the heart of medieval trading routes. It is the architecture of this period – mature Venetian Gothic – that for many visitors now encapsulates the image of Venice, and was to be revived by the Venetians themselves in the late 19th and early 20th centuries when seeking to rekindle former glories.

For Venice, trading with the East was often a delicate political tightrope. By the 11th century the Eastern Roman Empire was weakening and Turkish armies occupied the Holy Land. A succession of crusades was being mounted from Europe to physically rout the Turkish occupation. On top of the physical dangers and disruption that this presented to trade, the Pope would periodically issue sanctions against trade with the 'infidel'. Throughout, however, Venetian commerce prospered – if not through trading goods, then by supplying ships and resources to the crusading forces. Most infamous, and of considerable effect on the future fortunes and architecture of Venice, was the role that it played in the fourth crusade at the beginning of the 13th century. Having agreed huge sums for the provision of ships for the enterprise, it was found that the crusading forces lacked the means to pay Venice's costs in full. The solution, at Venice's persuasion, was that the crusade, while en-route to the Holy Land, should take Constantinople – on the pretext of bringing stability to the fractured Byzantine Empire. The battle was a bloody massacre, the result of which was that almost a third of the Empire was ceded to Venetian control. Venice thus gained a series of safe trading ports – a basis for the Republic's future power – and stripped Constantinople of its riches for relocation in Venice, most famously the four bronze horses mounted on the façade of San Marco, but also many lesser pieces of sculpture and architectural features incorporated in Venetian buildings.

For the next 300 years the now fully independent Republic, beholden to neither East nor West, would increasingly strengthen its position, establishing Venetian trading communities throughout the eastern Mediterranean and effecting trade in both goods and culture. One lasting legacy would be the unique style of Venetian architecture. Venice's pre-eminent position would not be seriously threatened until challenged by Spain and Portugal through their discovery of America and the eastern sea-trade routes via the Cape of Good Hope at the end of the 15th century.

Architecture and government

Much of Venice's strength lay in its government, a unique form that seamlessly bound individual and state together, a virtual Venice Inc. So impressive was its stability – the envy of many contemporary cities – that the traditionally feuding medieval Florence dubbed it *La Serenissima* (the Most Serene), an accolade that became the Republic's watchword. La Serenissima was a oligarchy. Its head – the doge – was elected for life but, being unfailingly old at that point, the incumbent rarely lived more than a few years. Although thought of as a figurehead rather than a political figure, a doge could nevertheless be highly influential. He was drawn from one of the great Venetian noble families. It was only the nobility in Venice who were permitted to hold office in the government, including the powerful grand council. The nobility consisted of 130 clans, a list of which was drawn up and then closed in 1297. It effectively remained closed until the fall of the Republic to Napoleon 500 years later. From time to time, however – usually reflecting a run on the Republic's coffers due to war, or, increasingly in the latter days, a fall in trade income – new wealthy families were able to buy their way in.

Architecture and political ambition

Progression of architectural styles in Venice largely mirrored advances in mainland Europe, albeit always with a uniquely Venetian twist based on eastern influence. However, the Venetian government was inherently conservative, jealously protecting its stability and wary of change which, in architecture, ensured that stylistic change came slowly. At the same time, despite its wealth and power, Venice was acutely aware that it was considered an arriviste, ostentatious society, lacking the gravitas that it needed to be diplomatically accepted. Until recently, scholars believed that Venice lacked a true Roman history, which no amount of looting of Roman artefacts from the adjacent mainland or from the East could provide. Current research, however, is questioning this assumption and presenting evidence of a Roman settlement on Torcello, which may have been virtually a suburb of Altino.

Then in 1453, with Constantinople falling to the Turk, Venice set about taking on the mantle of its natural successor – the new Rome. Built in 1460, the triumphal arch land gate to the Arsenale, rich in classical architectural language, heralds this shift. However, it was the election of Doge Andrea Gritti in 1523 that would lead to the so-called Romanisation of Venice's image. He immediately set about fostering close political and cultural links with Rome through enlightened artistic and architectural patronage. In 1527 Rome fell to the northern Hapsburg Empire, thus further opening the void that Venice wished to fill. It was Jacopo Sansovino – a refugee from the sack of Rome appointed by Gritti – who would finally give physical form to the Republic's ambition through his proposals for the Piazza San Marco. A series of Roman-style grand houses by Sansovino, starting with Palazzo Corner della Ca' Grande, would similarly transform the architecture of the Grand Canal.

Venice's ever-grander Renaissance and baroque architecture of the 16th and 17th centuries proclaimed fabulous wealth and continuing power. The political reality, however, was very different. No longer holding a monopoly on trade, and impoverished by wars – largely unsuccessful – Venice's fortune and influence was falling. Its days of great power and exploitation had won it few friends, and by the 18th century it was a marginalised state, primarily noted for its hedonistic lifestyle. When, in 1797, Napoleon entered the city it fell without resistance; a thousand years of the Venetian Republic was over.

Architecture and patronage

The history of architecture in Venice is tied not just to the civic pride of the government, but also to the commissioning power of the hugely influential *scuole grandi*, *scuole piccole* and trade guilds, the Church and monastic institutions, and a number of wealthy individuals intent on improving their grand houses.

The *scuole grandi* commisioned some of the greatest architects working in the city – including Pietro Lombardo, Mauro Codussi, Jacopo Sansovino – to enhance their buildings, particularly the façades (their faces to the world), and reflect their importance in the running of the city. Originating in the 13th century, by the end of the Republic there were seven *scuole grandi*. They developed into philanthropic institutions, raising funds, looking after members who fell on hard times, performing charitable works and meeting for prayer. Anyone from any sector of society could join, except clerics, and hundreds did, around 600 members in each of the larger *scuole*. Since no member of the nobility could hold office, it was in the *scuole* that some of the great merchant families (those not in the patriciate, and therefore barred from government office) were able to wield power. Although the *scuole* were supposedly collectively intent on enhancing the reputation of Venice itself, a certain rivalry existed between them, which was to result in the creation of some architectural masterpieces.

The plan of each *scuola* was similar, reflecting its usage. Its heart, always on the first floor, was the *albergo*, a small room, usually richly decorated, where the officers met and where particular treasures belonging to the organisation were kept. It is in its *albergo*, for instance, that the Scuola Grande di San Giovanni Evangelista still keeps the relic of the True Cross, the acquisition of which enhanced its status a hundredfold. Also on the first floor, but much larger, was the *sala capitolare* (chapter hall), which could accommodate all members for general meetings, voting or prayer. The chapter hall would often be architecturally rich, perhaps decorated with paintings by famous artists. That of the Scuola Grande di San Rocco, for instance, is a huge, imposing room decorated entirely with Tintoretto's specially commissioned paintings. Below this, often joined by an impressive staircase, was the *androne*, a plainer room, frequently colonnaded to support the floor of the chapter hall. *Scuola grande* building programmes were to face increasing criticism, on the grounds that more money was being spent on self-aggrandisement than on charity.

The *scuole piccole* were similar to *scuole grandi*, although more modest in scale with, typically, about 70 members. They often represented particular ethnic or religious groups within the city. Encouraged in their activities by the Franciscan and Dominican orders, they were often linked to monastic organisations helping orphans or disadvantaged people. Some of the more important *scuole piccole* buildings still survive. The Scuola di San Giorgio degli Schiavoni (home of the Dalmatians) can be visited, and its internal layout appreciated, though its chief attraction is not its architecture but the series of Carpaccio paintings still in situ.

Lastly, the trade guilds, slightly different to the *scuole piccole* in that they represented particular crafts rather than ethnic groups, also distributed alms, looked after poorer members, paid for funerals and so on. The Scuola dei Calegheri (shoemakers) in Campo San Tomà, and the Scuola dei Battjoro next to the church of San Stae, are two attractive examples which survive.

In addition to commissioning architects and artists to embellish their own buildings, the *scuole* and trade guilds were also crucially important to the legacy of interior church art and architecture in Venice. By commissioning altar pieces and their surrounds, which together might form the nucleus of a chapel dedicated to the Virgin or a particular saint associated with the confraternity, they demonstrated religious fervour while achieving kudos for their own organisation.

Between them, the *scuole* and the trade guilds embraced more or less the whole population of Venice, and demonstrated the tendency of Venetians to think and act collectively rather than individually. The notion of *mediocritas*, whereby no individual should set himself above another, was very powerful and contributed to the smooth running of the Republic. Almost inevitably, perhaps, *mediocritas* was more prevalent in some eras than others and certain individuals throughout the history of the Republic found ways to sidestep it. Baroque church façades (such as Santa Maria del Giglio), commissioned and paid for by an individual or a family, can be read as flamboyant architectural advertisements for status and importance. Similarly a wealthy individual building an elaborate palace on the Grand Canal might inscribe a dedication of the building to the city, but add their own name, carved in stone, for all to see.

It is worth noting that although many great houses are termed *palazzi* (palaces) today, only the doge's residence traditionally held this title. All others were *case grandi*, their splendour reinforcing, but subservient to, the international standing of the Republic, and certainly not intended to proclaim the importance of the owning family. This notion was increasingly flouted in the closing years of the Republic.

Patronage and the Church

The Church itself was a patron *par excellence*. Apart from San Marco itself, almost all the churches in Venice were either monastic foundations (founded largely by the Benedictines, Franciscans or Dominicans), parish churches or, occasionally, votive churches. Santa Maria della Salute, built to commemorate the end of a bout of plague, is an example of the third group. The Frari was the flagship church of the Franciscans, and Santi Giovanni e Paolo its counterpart for the Dominicans; many other important churches in the city were offshoots of these two parents. Whereas parish churches typically depended on a few noble families to support them, the monastic churches were often supported by the wealthiest Venetian patricians. Hence the Frari and Santi Giovanni e Paolo contain important monuments to numerous doges, and the tombs of the grandest Venetian families, executed by the leading architects, sculptors and artists of the day. Similarly commissioned were fine church façades and portals. Overall, the need for the great religious foundations to provide not only churches but also buildings to accommodate their monks' prayer, sleep, study, meeting and sustenance gave huge impetus to Venice's architectural townscape.

The Venetian merchant's house

The earliest great houses of Venice were built for trade. Their patrons – the wealthy merchant families of Venice – would, over the centuries, determine much of the appearance of the city through the constant updating and replication of houses for the various branches of each family. From the outset these buildings accommodated the merchant families – incorporating long open water frontages enabling the loading/unloading and storage of goods at ground level, and livi ng accommodation on first floor. Symbolic of Venice's abiding desire to distance itself from its Italian mainland neighbours, their layout and style looked to eastern precedent – building types that would have been familiar to Venetian traders doing business in Constantinople, Syria and Egypt. (Surviving early examples include the 12th-century Ca' Loredan and Farsetti and 13th-century Ca' da Mosto and Fondaco dei Turchi, the latter now rebuilt.) Their layout was tripartite, incorporating a large central room flanked by ancillary accommodation – a plan form that continued largely unchanged through the centuries regardless of changing architectural style. Main façades – seen at their most consistently impressive on the Grand Canal – became Venice's decorative window on the world, emblematic individually of the owning family's wealth, and collectively proclaiming the power and culture of the Republic. The main façade, with its characteristic open arcading and windows, created a relatively lightweight screen that minimised loading on the foundations. Crucial to its practicality was access to large quantities of cheaply produced window glazing from the furnaces of Murano.

Construction techniques

The watchwords of Venetian construction were (and remain) lightness, even loading and flexibility. The primary building material used was brick, layed using a weak lime-based mortar to allow movement without cracking. Marble and stone – increasingly used to face the grander buildings – was rarely more than a thin veneer over brick. Vaulted ceilings and domes are rare in Venice for the very reason that their construction is intolerant to movement. Where vaulting was used – for example in the great Gothic churches of Santi Giovanni e Paolo and the Frari – it is strutted across with timber beams. Much more typical is the flat timber-beamed ceiling. A particularly beautiful Venetian church roof form is the ship's keel – so-called because it looks like an inverted hull. It is thought to have derived from the city's ship-building tradition; an excellent example can be seen at the church of Santo Stefano.

By the 14th century a standard technique had been perfected which ensured the firmest possible base for construction. A building's foundations had to reach the hard bed of clay which lies 3–5 metres below water level. Timber piles, typically of larch or oak, were driven down through the upper levels of sand and soft clay. The piles were tightly packed (1.2 million are said to underpin the Salute) to form a solid timber base, effectively lifting the clay bearing level, which was then further consolidated with a double layer of planks cemented in place. (Unless exposed to air, this timber does not decay over centuries.) Construction of the building itself would then typically start with several courses of Istrian stone as foundation and a defence against rising damp, before reverting to brickwork.

Construction of the great houses fronting the canals was such that the main façade was little more than a self-supporting stage set that could be perforated, modified, updated or entirely replaced without fundamentally compromising the stability of the overall building. Many of today's façades present a patchwork of such alteration.

Post-Republican Venice

With the fall of the Republic, Napoleon quickly set about dismantling its traditional mechanisms of government. At the political heart – the Piazza San Marco – Napoleon planned a grand royal palace, part of which – the Ala Napoleonica – can be seen today. San Marco itself, formerly the doge's private chapel – was designated to be Venice's cathedral. To counter insurgence within the ordinary populace, many churches were deconsecrated and *scuole* closed, breaking the tight structure of traditional Venetian life. This was clearly the end of the line, and many of the leading Venetian families soon left the city, abandoning their great houses whose fate, as noted by Ruskin, was frequently to fall into dereliction. Within 50 years the first link to the mainland – the railway causeway – was built. Venice's period of occupation – initially by the French, subsequently by the Austrians – was to last until 1866, shortly after which it became a part of the newly created kingdom of Italy.

For many years the city had been effectively bankrupt. It has been estimated that by 1820 a quarter of the population was reduced to begging. Attempts to revive Venice's financial fortunes initially looked to industrialisation – the architectural legacy of which can be found in the outlying areas of Sestiere di Santa Croce, Murano and the Giudecca. More successful was to be Venice's late-19th-century ambition to become a leading tourist and cultural destination, leading to the development of the Lido and the instigation of the Biennale festivals. So successful in fact that tourism is now Venice's major commercial activity.

Ruskin and Venice

Writer, critic and lecturer John Ruskin's detailed architectural study and record of Venice, *The Stones of Venice* (1851–53), coupled with his powerful and articulate championing of the city and its plight, still colour the views of visitors to the Lagoon. While his preoccupations and prejudices – particularly those concerning the superiority of Gothic architecture over Renaissance and baroque – may now seem backward looking, and while more balanced commentaries including, we hope, this guide, are now available, the passion and force of his views remain unsurpassed. For this reason, they are frequently quoted.

The geography of Venice

The historic centre of Venice, focused on the serpentine route of the Grand Canal, is made up of more than 100 islands defined by a network of waterways. It comprises six administrative districts termed *sestieri* (sixths) – Cannaregio, San Marco and Castello to the north, Dorsoduro, Santa Croce and San Polo to the south. At its heart is the Sestiere di San Marco, historically the point of arrival by sea, from which the layout of Venice radiates. It held the political and commercial power of the Republic from the Piazza San Marco to the Rialto. To the east lies Castello, former home to the vast shipbuilding yards of the Arsenale and root of Venice's maritime strength, and the church of San Pietro di Castello – Venice's cathedral until this function was relocated to the basilica of San Marco. To the west, San Polo – south of the Grand Canal and over the Rialto bridge – was home to the Republic's trading centre and main markets.

Today's visitor by rail or car will first see Venice from arrival at its western fringes in Cannaregio and Santa Croce. Remote from the traditional heart of the city's splendour, even today they remain less densely developed.

THE ISLANDS Immediately to the north of the *sestieri* lies the island of San Michele – Venice's cemetery (site of British architect David Chipperfield's 1998 competition-winning proposals for extension but, at the time of writing, still a long way from completion). Beyond, into the northern Lagoon, the islands of Murano, Burano and Torcello have all provided shelter since the earliest days of the Lagoon's inhabitation. In particular, the importance of Torcello pre-dates the rise of Venice. Its churches of Santa Maria Assunta and Santa Fosca, founded in the early 7th century under the Roman emperor Heraclius, whose seat was in Constantinople, were once at the heart of a thriving community. Today they stand in eerie isolation. As Venice's fortunes rose from the 9th century onwards, so Torcello's declined, such that by the 13th century its buildings would be largely demolished and relocated to Venice and their materials reused on the main island.

GIUDECCA In the 16th century, as Venice's centre became increasingly intensively developed, humanist renaissance ideals were highlighting the shortcomings of a wholly urban life. The Venetian nobility looked to the Giudecca on which to build 'country' retreats – Renaissance villas with extensive gardens. Although little evidence of these remains, more modest domestic housing of the period survives, as do two Palladian churches – the Redentore and Zitelle – which look back to Dorsoduro from the waterfront. Ironically, today's architectural legacy, far from pastoral idyll, is largely of Venice's ultimately doomed attempt to industrialise in the 19th and early 20th centuries – now-derelict factories and mass-housing. Recently, however, the island has become the setting for a series of redevelopment and refurbishment programmes, chiefly providing housing, and it is some of the best of these that this guide describes.

THE LIDO Until the late 19th century, the Lido remained almost undeveloped – its role in the days of the Republic being as a shield against the Adriatic. Then came the advent of

INTRODUCTION

organised tourism and Venice's intention to establish itself as a major holiday destination. The development which followed was not subject to the constraints of the centre of Venice – roads and cars substitute for canals and boats – and today it demonstrates a wealth of private villa and hotel design in both revivalist and contemporary 20th-century style.

The future of Venice

The city of Venice has been in decline for more than 300 years, its dilemma vastly predating contemporary society's concern to revitalise post-industrial cities. Mass tourism can never substitute for a vital thriving community and may yet reduce the city to no more than a theme park. Since the Second World War Venice's population has halved and it continues to decline. Because of high property prices, such private residential development as is taking place, for instance restoration of buildings on the Giudecca, is typically being sold to non-Venetians. Much contemporary public-sector housing is in the outlying areas. Architecturally, the city centre has remained conservative, with a predominance of revivalist work looking back to the glorious days of the Republic. An international campaign for the protection of the urban fabric of Venice, formalised in the mid 1960s, has meant that while exemplary restoration continues to take place, all new development proposals in the central area have been ultimately rejected.

Such caution is understandable. While frustrating for Venetian architects, most of whom have to work elsewhere in Italy or indeed abroad, it is not a modern phenomenon – in the past, Jacopo Sansovino, Palladio, Le Corbusier and Frank Lloyd Wright are just some of the big names who have fallen foul of the city's view of itself. Venice has at different periods embraced change, but only so much, and not enough to impinge on the city's particular brand of civic pride.

This guide considers those areas – the islands of the Lagoon and the Lido – traditionally associated with the heart of Venice, and the destination for most visitors. However, the coming years should see the fruition of a range of development proposals for the mainland area of Mestre and the industrialised zone around Porto Marghera, which may help to revitalise the overall dynamic of the city. To date, the most architecturally visible of these is the Science Park (architects Wilhelm Holzbauer with Paolo Piva and Roberto Sordina) located at the approach to the road and rail crossing.

Venice's challenge at the beginning of the 21st century remains how to rebuild a balanced and vital society.

HOW TO USE THIS BOOK

Our selection of buildings, and commentary on them, is primarily intended to provide an insight into the socio-political history of Venice, and the central role that architecture has played in capturing and reflecting the fortunes of the city. This approach requires a representative balance, so that the reader will find not just (and certainly not all) the show-stopping creations of the city's heyday, but also the modest and everyday. We have followed the history of Venice from its origins, through the great days of its wealth, into its decadence, fall and longed-for rebirth. Nineteenth- and 20th-century buildings account for more than a third of the guide. While inevitably some may not stand the test of time, they are a testament to the Venetians' enduring ambition to forge a future from their extraordinary architectural history.

The narrow labyrinthine nature of Venice's centre, the lack of long-distance views for orientation and the serpentine form of its main waterway – the Grand Canal – can be a challenge to the visitor. Venice works in *sestieri* – districts. Each has its own numbering system, which can seem neither logical nor apparent. One of our guiding principles has been to locate each building accurately. However, in addition, a good indexed map – for example, the readily available *Venezia* produced by Studio F.M.B. Bologna – is essential. Since all Venetian maps are indexed according to *sestieri* we have followed that convention in laying out this book. The practical shortcoming of this approach is that, on the ground, the boundaries are effectively invisible, and so the visitor – merely referring to one *sestiere*'s building list – could miss a virtually adjacent listing from the next *sestiere*. Hopefully the schematic map in this book will help.

The naming of an individual *palazzo* or *Ca'* (short for *Casa*) can lead to confusion. Firstly, although often termed *palazzi* (palaces) today, only the doge's residence traditionally held this title. All others were a *casa* or *casa grande*. Secondly, although typically named after their historic owners, ownership has usually changed over the years – the grand families relocating and splitting through intermarriage. Accordingly some family names – such the Corner, Contarini, Loredan and Falier – recur in different combinations in several locations in the city. We have tried to identify the most common unique naming for each.

All buildings have been given their relevant *vaporetto* stop. In the centre this is primarily as an additional location aid, since the best way to get around is really on foot. Cross-references are included where comparisons are thought useful. In the case of those buildings fronting the Grand Canal we have also identified viewpoints from the opposite bank so that façades may be viewed at leisure rather than from the heaving mass of a *vaporetto*. Where relevant, opening times are given and, where necessary, details of whom to contact to gain access to interiors. Things can change, however, and a visit to the helpful tourist information centre that is currently in the neoclassical coffee house in *sestiere* San Marco is recommended.

SCAFFOLDING The restoration and maintenance of Venice's architectural heritage are never-ending tasks; a building's façade can suddenly disappear under scaffolding and remain 'wrapped' for months or even years. At the time of writing – though not of photography – all the buildings featured in this guide were unscaffolded. If this is not the case when using the guide, take consolation that some other previously hidden masterpiece will have been restored and now be visible.

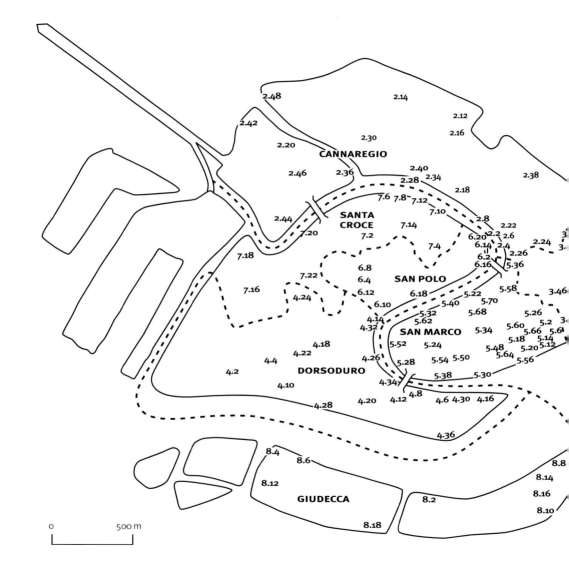

CANNAREGIO

2.48
2.14
2.12
2.42
2.16
2.30
2.20
2.46
2.36
2.40
2.34
2.38
2.28
2.18
2.44
SANTA CROCE
7.6 7.8 7.12
7.10
2.8
2.22
7.20
7.14
2.2 2.6
2.24
7.2
7.4
6.20
2.4
3.
7.18
6.14
2.26
3.
6.2
5.36
6.16
7.22
6.8
SAN POLO
5.58
3.46
6.4
6.18
5.22
7.16
6.12
5.70
4.24
6.10
5.40
5.68
5.26
4.14
5.32
5.2 3
4.32
5.62
SAN MARCO
5.34
5.60
5.6
4.18
5.52
5.24
5.18
5.14
4.22
4.26
5.48
5.20 5.12
4.4
5.28
5.54 5.50
5.64 5.56
4.2
DORSODURO
5.38
5.30
4.10
4.34
4.20
4.12 4.8
4.6 4.30 4.16
4.28
4.36

8.4
8.6
8.8
8.12
8.14
8.16
GIUDECCA
8.2
8.10
8.18

o   500 m

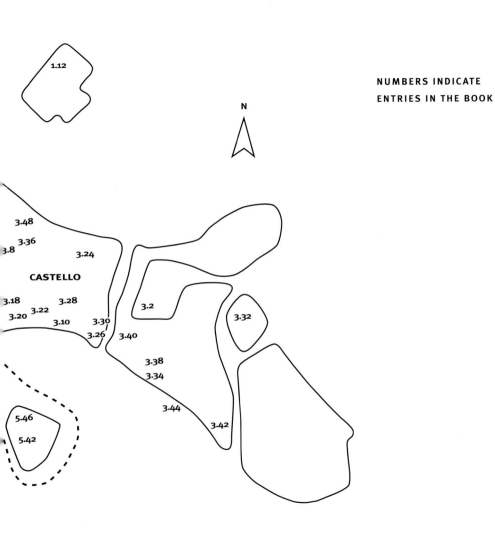

1.12

NUMBERS INDICATE
ENTRIES IN THE BOOK

N

3.48
3.36
3.8
3.24

CASTELLO

3.18
3.28
3.20 3.22
3.10
3.30
3.26
3.40
3.2
3.32
3.38
3.34
3.44
3.42

5.46
5.42

HOW TO USE THIS BOOK

VENICE: AN ARCHITECTURAL GUIDE

Buildings on the Grand Canal	Viewpoints
Cannaregio	
CA' DA MOSTO	FABBRICHE NUOVE, SAN POLO
CA' D'ORO	PESCHERIA, SAN POLO
PALAZZO LOREDAN-VENDRAMIN-CALERGI	DEPOSITO DEL MEGIO, SANTA CROCE
Dorsoduro	
CA' DARIO	CAMPO TRAGHETTO, NEAR SANTA MARIA DEL GIGLIO, SAN MARCO
PALAZZO CONTARINI DAL ZAFFO	PONTE DELL'ACCADEMIA
PALAZZO BALBI	CALLE GIUSTINIAN, DORSODURO
PALAZZO STERN	SAN SAMUELE TRAGHETTO STOP, SAN MARCO
CASA SALVIATI	CAMPO TRAGHETTO, NEAR SANTA MARIA DEL GIGLIO, SAN MARCO
San Marco	
CA' FARSETTI/CA' LOREDAN	FONDAMENTA SAN SILVESTRO, SAN POLO
PALAZZO FALIER CANOSSA	CAMPO DELLA CARITÀ (ACCADEMIA), DORSODURO

SELECT BIBLIOGRAPHY

In the compilation of this guide we particularly wish to thank the authors of the following scholarly works:

Brown, Patricia Fortini, *Venice and Antiquity*, Yale University Press, 1996

Concina, Ennio, *A History of Venetian Architecture*, Cambridge University Press, 1998

Goy, Richard, *Venice – the city and its architecture*, Phaidon, 1997

Hills, Paul, *Venetian Colour*, Yale University Press, 1999

Howard, Deborah, *Venice and The East*, Yale University Press, 2000

Lieberman, Ralph, *Renaissance Architecture in Venice* (Becocci Editore), Frederick Muller Ltd, 1982

Romanelli, Giandomenico (ed.), *Venice – Art & Architecture*, Könemann, 1997

Other works consulted and acknowledged include:

Littlewood, Ian, *Venice: A Literary Companion*, John Murray, 1991

Maretto, Paolo, *Venezia – Architettura Del XX Secolo*, Vitali & Ghianda, nd (1960s)

Mazzariol, G and Dorigato, A, *Venetian Palazzi*, Taschen, 1998

De Michelis, Marco (ed.), *Venezia – La Nuova Architettura*, Skira, 1999

Morris, James, *Venice*, Faber & Faber, 1960

Pizzarello, U and Capitano, E, *Guida Alla Citta di Venezia*, L'Altra Riva, 1986–89

Quill, Sarah, *Ruskin's Venice – The Stones Revisited*, Ashgate Publishing, 2000

Salvadori, R and Rossi, T B, *Venice – Guide to Sculpture from its Origins to the 20th Century*, Canal & Stamperia Editrice, 1997

Trincanato, Egle, *Venetian Domestic Architecture*, Canal & Stamperia Editrice, 1998

Zucconi, Guido, *Venice – an architectural guide,* Arsenale Editrice, 1993

GLOSSARY

ALBERGO upper-level small meeting room in a *scuola*, used by its officials

ALTANA roof terrace, usually raised above the tiled roofs

ANDRONE main ground floor hall of Venetian *palazzo* or *scuola*

APSE semi-circular or polygonal domed recess off church nave

BALDACCHINO canopy supported on columns, usually over an altar or tomb

BARBARI MAP Jacopo de' Barbari's meticulous woodcut of 1500 (now in the Correr Museum) recording the architecture of Venice at that time

BAROQUE developed from mannerism, an exuberant and theatrical interpretation and application of classical design features

BASILICA a plan form adopted by the earliest Christian churches. Based on the Roman hall of justice, it is a simple single colonnaded space, typically with parallel side aisles, focused on an apse at one end

BAS-RELIEF shallow-carved projecting sculptural ornamentation

BYZANTINE originating in the Eastern Roman Empire based in Constantinople, the style grows out of late-Roman and Greek architectural conventions but abandons the classical rigour of the Orders. Developed into the so-called Romanesque style in Europe, its Venetian incarnation – Veneto-Byzantine – is a unique mix with greater eastern influence

BYZANTIUM Greek name for today's Istanbul, renamed Constantinople by the Roman emperor Constantine

CALLE secondary street

CAMPANILE bell tower

CAMPIELLO small square

CAMPO square

CARENA DI NAVE translated as 'ship's keel roof', a form of church roof reminiscent of an upturned ship's keel, thought to utilise skills and technologies developed through Venice's ship-building industry

CHANCEL the liturgical, traditionally eastern end of a church for use by those who officiate during services

CHAPTER HALL the large upstairs room in a

GLOSSARY

scuola used for meetings of the membership and for holding masses

CLERESTORY high-level window/glazed storey, typically in a church

CLOISTER covered monastic walkway around three or four sides of a quadrangle for access to adjoining accommodation and study

CORTE housing courtyard

CUPOLA a small drum finishing a roof dome or tower

DENTIL/DENTILATION Venetian Gothic decorative moulding in stone/brick in the form of small cubic projections alternating on either side of a central line; typically seen around window and door openings. A Moorish feature adopted by the Venetians

DOGE the elected leader of the Venetian Republic (Venetian dialect from the Latin *dux*)

ENTABLATURE upper part of an order of architecture, comprising architrave, frieze, and cornice

EXTRADOS the outer curve of an arch

FINIAL an ornate termination, such as to a pinnacle or spire

FONDACO warehouse or store

FONDAMENTA the public quayside along a canal

GOTHIC an architectural style rooted in northern Europe, taking little from Greek and Roman classical architectural traditions, characterised by the pointed arch and, as time went on, increasingly elaborately traceried windows. It contrasts the largely static simple column-and-beam construction of classical architecture with soaring, light-filled space. As a complete building system, little seen in Venice due to the difficulties of building in the Lagoon. Venetian Gothic – for many the defining architectural style of the city – displays a unique adaptation of Gothic principles

GREEK CROSS applied to the layout of a church, this is a centralised cross where each arm is of the same length. It reflects and accommodates liturgical practices commonly associated with eastern Christianity

ICONOSTASIS the screen separating chancel from nave in Orthodox Christian churches

KEYSTONE the crowning piece of an arch that holds the whole in place

LOGGIA an open recess, typically colonnaded or arcaded, at ground or *piano-nobile* level

LATIN CROSS applied to the layout of a church, this adopts the form of a crucifix where the stem – the nave – is longer than the other three arms, reflecting European Christian practice

LUNETTE a semi-circular window or wall-panel let into the inner base of a vault or dome

MANNERISM the use of classical design features, but in increasingly unconventional ways that depart from the strict rules of classicism. Later developing into baroque

MARMORINO a final wall render coat containing crushed marble capable of being polished to give a fine marble-like surface

MEDIOCRITAS the governing principle, increasingly circumvented in the closing years of the Republic, that, to ensure political stability, no individual citizen should use wealth or influence to put themselves above the state

NEOCLASSICISM a reaction against the architectural excess of baroque and an attempt to recapture the true spirit of classical architecture. It questioned the former Renaissance interpretations, taking an empirical approach strictly based on archaeological evidence to produce frequently severe designs

OCULUS a circular wall opening, window or panel

OGEE an S-shaped double curve

ORDER an assembly of parts consisting of a column, its base and capital, and entablature, all proportioned and decorated consistent with one of the so-called orders – Doric, Tuscan, Ionic, Corinthian and composite, stemming from the measured observation of classical Greek and Roman architecture

PATERAE flat circular, saucer-like ornamentation of stone or marble

PIANO NOBILE the main floor of a building, containing its most important reception rooms, typically with a greater ceiling height and marked by a grand expression on the façade

PILASTER rectangular wall-projection mimicking the detail of a column

PILOTI posts on an unenclosed ground floor carrying a raised building

PORTEGO the great ceremonial first-floor hall of Venetian *palazzi*

GLOSSARY

PORTICO a colonnade space forming a covered anteroom/entrance

PRONAOS similar to portico, but applied specifically to a temple

QUATREFOIL a Gothic ornament of three-foils/ arcs each separated from the next by a cusp (typically in an arch)

RENAISSANCE literally a rebirth – the rediscovery and application of the design principles found in classical Greek and Roman architecture – but, in fact, a reinterpretation of such principles. Later questioned by neoclassicism.

RIO secondary canal

RIO TERRÀ former canal, now infilled

RUSTICATION Renaissance device employing stones dressed in high relief, often with exaggerated jointing, plain or rough surfaced, to give the appearance of massive impregnability, typically to the lower storey

SALIZZADA main street, paved from earliest time

SERLIANA composite window, comprising a large central arched opening flanked by lesser rectangular openings

LA SERENISSIMA The Most Serene [Republic] – the name by which the Venetian Republic was traditionally known

SOTOPÒRTEGO a covered passageway or collonade with building over

STILTED (ARCH) an elongated arch with vertical sides

STUCCO a plaster finish, inside or out, typically moulded and ornamented

TAMBOUR the drum of a column or wall of a cupola

TRAGHETTO the traditional, and still extant, public gondola ferry service across the Grand Canal at various points

TREFOIL a Gothic ornament of three foils/arcs each separated from the next by a cusp (typically in an arch)

ACKNOWLEDGEMENTS

This guide would not have been possible without the kindness and support of numerous Venetian individuals and organisations. In particular we are pleased to thank the Azienda Promozione Turistica, Chorus: Associazone Chiese di Venezia, Fondazione Querini Stampalia, Roberto Sordina, Serena Maffioletti, Gianni Morra, Rosella Cargasacchi, Elisa Di Cataldo, Cesare Battisti, Nedo Fiorentin, Valeriano Pastor, Erica Zecca, Giovanni Girolimetto and Edda Lisa Basaldella of RAI at the Palazzo Labia, Giorgio Bonnetto at Hotel Ungaria, Sasa Dobricic and Alessandro Marchi. Special thanks are due to Richard Goy, author of *Venice – the city and its architecture* (Phaidon, 1997), for his invaluable comments on the proofs of this book.

THE ISLANDS

TORCELLO
SANTA MARIA ASSUNTA, SANTA FOSCA

This tiny, peaceful island, now peopled only by tourists and those who provide for them, was once a flourishing community, inhabited by early settlers in the Lagoon. In the 7th century, when the Lombards were advancing, people from the shoreline Roman city of Altino, where the bishopric had been relocated from Aquileia, fled to the swamps and marshes. Their bishop came too, and Torcello developed into a important community of 20,000 people, declining only in the 13th century with the growth of Venice, the silting up of nearby channels and the onset of malaria.

SANTA MARIA ASSUNTA, the cathedral, was rebuilt in the 9th century, but today's simple basilica plan, an early Christian model and stylistically a development of nearby Grado cathedral, dates from a major reconstruction, largely with Altino stone, in 1008. The exterior is severe, made more so by the unique stone-shuttered windows on the south façade. The interior, however, is bathed in light and colour. The green Greek marble columns are capped with delicate Corinthian capitals, the pinkish brickwork is clean and light, and the intricate 11th-century mosaic floor newly restored.

While the plan of the church is Roman, the mosaics, some of which may have been executed by the same artists who worked at San Marco, are from the Byzantine tradition, which greatly influenced Venetian art and architecture. (Constantinople, previously the Greek City of Byzantium, was then home of the Roman Emperor, to whom the Lagoon owed allegiance.) A frightening mosaic of the Last Judgement fills the west wall, and over the apse is the story of the Annunciation and Nativity with, in the centre, the Madonna and Child floating in a sea of gold. Another highlight is the 11th-century rood screen, delicately carved with flowers and birds.

The church was once connected to the 7th-century Baptistry – the remains are in front

7th–11th centuries

TORCELLO

of the basilica – fashioned on the design of Roman thermal baths. Much of the rest of Torcello was eventually dismantled and used as building material elsewhere in the Lagoon.

SANTA FOSCA's portico, thought to have been added in the 12th century, has an open colonnade, with Veneto-Byzantine brick arches supported on Greek marble columns. It provides a peaceful, intermediate space on five sides of the church. The interior has been much restored, but the bare brick walls and Greek marble columns with decorative Corinthian capitals evoke the simple piety of the first settlers. Santa Fosca has a centralised Greek-cross plan with a short nave and projecting arms. This was a common plan in the Eastern Empire. Along with the basilica, which developed into the Latin coss, the Greek cross and its variations were to be used extensively in Venetian churches. The patterned brickwork on the walls of the apse itself can also be seen at Santi Maria e Donato on Murano and San Marco itself. Santa Fosca is not domed, but has a timber roof.

Two views of Santa Fosca should not be missed: one from the first floor of the interesting museum opposite, and the other from the recently restored brick campanile of the basilica – a vista that includes the watery landscape of the Lagoon.

THE ISLANDS

LOCATION from the landing stage walk along a peaceful canal, past the Ponte del Diavolo
VAPORETTO Torcello. Boats from Fondamente Nuove and waterfront by the Palazzo Ducale – or take a one-day boat trip round all the islands
ACCESS tickets for the complex on sale 10.30–17.30, last entry 17.00. These times change according to the season, so check at the tourist office

11th century

MURANO
SANTI MARIA E DONATO, PALAZZO DA MULA

The charming tourist trap of Murano was, like Torcello, first settled by the Altinese fleeing the Lombard invasions on the mainland. Unlike malaria-infested Torcello, it remained economically important long after the rise of Venice itself. By the 10th century it had become a thriving community with considerable independence, its own mint and judiciary. The population soared. The glass-blowing industry was transferred here in 1291 (considered a fire risk on the main island) and Murano glass quickly became an important export commodity. In the mid 15th century Murano was the home of Antonio Vivarini and his school of painters, but the island's heyday was the 16th century. By this time Murano had become a rural retreat for artists and literati, nobles and rich merchants escaping the bustle of Venice. The result was a cluster of fine palaces. landscaped gardens and orchards.

SANTI MARIA E DONATO, originally 7th century and dedicated to the Virgin, was reconstructed in 1140 and rededicated to San Donato after his remains and the bones of the dragon he killed (by spitting at it) were brought to Venice by Doge Domenico Michiel. Stylistically, the church forms a link between Santa Maria Assunta on Torcello and San Marco itself. The best view is from the canal, where the picturesque hexagonal apse commands the waterway like an elegant private palace. With its blind arches, Istrian stone columns and parapets, patterned brickwork and a band of ornament with five or six types of marble inlay (Ruskin called this a 'necklace of precious stones'), it is a fine example of the earliest Veneto-Byzantine architecture. The main façade is plain (a planned portico was never built) but inside, the mosaic floor, contemporary with those in San Marco, is a colourful tapestry of abstract patterns and symbolic figurative pictures. Dated 1141, it was relaid in the 1970s.

The basilical plan of Santa Maria Assunta has evolved here into a primitive Latin

7th century; reconstructed 1140 (restored 1973–79)

MURANO

cross with transepts, the nave separated from the aisles by Greek columns with Corinthian capitals, The wooden *carena di nave* (ship's keel) roof is traditionally Venetian (also, for example, at Santo Stefano and San Giacomo d'Orio, and see Introduction, page 0.16). A 13th-century polychrome altarpiece contains an image of San Donato and behind the altar are four alleged dragon bones. Note the fine 12th-century mosaic of the Virgin.

The adjacent baptistry was destroyed in 1719, but the 20th-century war memorial in the *campo* complements the church well. Nearby is the 12th-13th-century campanile.

LOCATION along the Fondamenta Giustinian which borders the Canale di San Donato
VAPORETTO Museo from Fondamente Nuove or waterfront by the Palazzo Ducale
ACCESS open daily, 8.00–12.00 and 16.00–19.00

PALAZZO DA MULA A few 14th-century houses and palazzos still exist on Murano, particularly along the Fondamenta dei Vetrai. Opposite the Ponte Longo/Vivarini is the Palazzo da Mula, which was refigured in the 16th century – a third storey was added and the façade altered – to provide a fine country home. Unusually, the palace is a detached square and can be seen from all four sides. Its design is symmetrical, the Istrian stone high-Gothic detailing elaborate and rather cramped, particularly on the *piano nobile*, where four roundels and two identical bas-reliefs crowd around the central four-light window.

LOCATION Fondamenta da Mula by the Ponte Longo (on some maps Ponte Vivarini), a walk along the Fondamenta dei Vetrai from the *vaporetto* stop
VAPORETTO Colonna/Museo (Murano)
ACCESS not open to the public

14th century (reworked 16th century)

SAN MICHELE
SAN MICHELE IN ISOLA

Before Napoleon picked the island of San Michele to become Venice's cemetery, it had, since the 10th century, been home to Camoldesi monks. Of their 15th-century church one observer wrote, 'You will see it and will be stunned, and your heart will rejoice'. Its architect – Mauro Codussi, only in his twenties at the time – took the familiar three-part Venetian Gothic form (seen, for example at San Giovanni in Bragora in Campo Bandiera e Moro, Castello) and developed it to create the first wholly Renaissance church in the city. This dazzling white façade is also the first example of complete stone cladding and presents a perfectly proportioned, balanced composition of textures and contrasting light and shade. The small hexagonal domed building to the left is the Emiliana chapel – a marble-lined, richly embellished treasure box or, if you agree with Ruskin's derogatory view, 'a German summer-house', providing a contrast to the refined detailing of Codussi. First built by Guglielmo dei Grigi Bergamasco in 1527, the chapel was renovated 30 years later by Sansovino. It is currently being restored by the Venice in Peril Fund.

Leaning precariously over the church is the Gothic campanile – a confection of carved brickwork and stone detailing. To the right a Gothic doorway leads through 15th-century cloisters to the extensive cemetery (19th century), although those searching for David Chipperfield's competition-winning new extension will, at the time of writing, be disappointed. Its realisation remains locked in Venetian bureaucracy.

VAPORETTO Cimitero
ACCESS church open daily, 7.30–12.15, 15.00–16.00; cemetery open daily, 7.30–18.00 (summer), 7.30–16.00 (winter)

Mauro Codussi/Jacopo Sansovino 1469–78

SOCIAL HOUSING ON MAZZORBO

In the early 1980s, Venice's then socialist administration instigated competitions for municipal housing in the Venetian pattern of canal and pavement, pedestrian streets and small squares. De Carlo's housing on Mazzorbo was an impressive result. Mazzorbo is connected to Burano by an attractive footbridge, and it is Burano's brightly coloured housing – originally the colours of the community's fishing boats – that De Carlo's housing reflects. The colour palette was originally limited to blue, yellow and violet, although new colours have now crept in. For De Carlo, such personalisation is a basic human need – 'to be in a boat, coming back, and to say to your friend, "my house is there, it's the blue one".'

For each of the 36 two- and three-storey houses in the first phase, living accommodation is at ground level, with doors leading directly from the front pavement and rear court. Bedrooms and terraces are above – a Buranese tradition. The whole is articulated using bays, projecting corners and stairtowers. The canal to the front was excavated and the connection from pavement to house effected by raising the site level – thus avoiding flooding.

The first phase is showing its age now: the metal guttering leaks so that the paintwork is stained and the mosaic decoration to the commercial units looks dated. The brighter, traditional houses of Burano, with their varying heights and volumes, seem to mock Mazzorbo's houses for being a pale imitation of the real thing. Nevertheless, this is a truly Venetian housing solution. Further stages are being built.

LOCATION linked by footbridge to the island of Burano
VAPORETTO Burano (from Fondamente Nuove). May deposit you back at San Zaccaria. Check, as island-hopping times and *vaporetto* stops vary according to the season. Or take a boat trip taking in all the islands from San Marco

Giancarlo de Carlo 1980s

CANNAREGIO

CA' DA MOSTO

In the 13th century, the decoration of Venetian palace façades began to show Byzantine influence. Slabs of precious marble replaced Aurisina stone (Istrian stone also made an appearance at this time), and carved *paterae* and acanthus-leaf or floral friezes were used as ornament. The Ca' da Mosto, one of the oldest palaces on the Grand Canal, is a good example of early Veneto-Byzantine design. Despite the picturesque, crumbling state of the building, you can clearly see the form and decoration of the lower two storeys. The extradoses of the open arches on the assymetrical lower storey are richly detailed, and the *piano nobile* is beautifully decorated with marble slabs, tiles, *paterae* and friezes. Originally highly coloured, the slabs above the six-light window show Christ on a throne raising his hand in blessing, flanked by intricately carved animals and floral decoration.

The palace was built as a residence and warehouse for the da Mosto family, merchants and members of the Venetian nobility, and the rich ornamentation points to the importance, and self-importance, of the owners. The palace remained unchanged until the 17th century, when the third floor and mezzanine were added. Alvise da Mosto (the first European to sail round Cape Verde, and discoverer of the Canary Islands) was born here in 1465. From the 16th to 17th centuries, the building was host to the Albergo del Leon Bianco (White Lion Hotel).

CANNAREGIO

LOCATION Grand Canal. Corte del Leon Bianco
VAPORETTO Rialto or Ca' d'Oro
ACCESS not open to the public
VIEWPOINT from the waterfront of the Fabbriche Nuove, on the opposite bank of the Grand Canal

13th century

CA' LION MOROSINI

Tucked away just a few metres from the main pedestrian drag as it passes San Giovanni Crisostomo is the Campiello Remer – originally the courtyard of the Ca' Lion Morosini, one of the earliest surviving Venetian great houses. The Lion family were refugees from the Syrian crusader capital of Acre, returning to Venice after the city's fall in 1291. In layout the building follows a plan typical throughout western Europe at that time – main accommodation on the first floor, with storage/warehousing beneath, and an external staircase giving access to the living quarters.

The house faces the Grand Canal, directly opposite the Fabbriche Nuove, but remains set back beyond the courtyard. This essentially utilitarian layout would shortly change as engineering advances coupled with the desire to display a frontage directly on to the water would result in the familiar Grand Canal 'show' façade with courtyard placed behind (as at Ca' Da Mosto, and see Introduction, pages 0.15 and 0.16). The overall architectural style is eclectic but eastern influence is very clear in the first-floor, Byzantine-arched entrance with its paired, flanking, ogee-arched windows in transition between Byzantine and Gothic style. The external staircase supported on massive Gothic arches perplexed Ruskin although other commentators have suggested that the style – rising off an initial flight of round arched supports – is rooted in the crusader architecture common in Acre. The fine courtyard wellhead is basically Romanesque but stylistically modified by the later addition of Gothic ogee detailing.

LOCATION Calle della Stua/Calle Remer, off Campo San Giovanni Crisostomo
VAPORETTO Ca' d'Oro/Rialto
ACCESS not open to the public

13th century

CA' FALIER

Fronting on to the Campo Santi Apostoli rather than the Grand Canal, this early great house, although much altered over the centuries, is an important survivor. It is contemporary with the adjacent Ca' da Mosto and shows architectural details of the transitional period between the Byzantine and Gothic – exemplified in the first-floor central windows. Here, although clearly truncated, the surviving four windows have the Byzantine round-headed stilted arches – as seen at the earlier Ca' Farsetti and Loredan – but their outer stone moulding is now a simple roll rising through an ogee to a point. The building is today completely absorbed into Venice's street pattern – its ground-floor quayside forming part of the busy route between Rialto and the railway station. Standing in this arcade is one of the Republic's traditional stone proclamation tablets – this one making it clear that no one other than a member of the bakers' guild may make or sell bread and listing penalties for infringement that range from a fine, through galley-work to prison or, indeed, hanging.

The building is also infamous for being home to Doge Marin Falier – instigator of a mid-14th-century plot to overthrow the Republic by killing off what he considered to be a decadent nobility and taking sole control. When the plot was discovered, he was immediately beheaded, and today is marked in the Palazzo Ducale gallery of doges merely by a black curtain and an equally direct inscription – '*Hic est locus Marini Falehri decapitati pro criminibus*'.

LOCATION Rio dei Santi Apostoli. While in the campo, take in the Capella Cornaro in the church of Santi Apostoli
VAPORETTO Ca' d'Oro
ACCESS not open to the public

13th century

CA' D'ORO

When Marin Contarini rebuilt the Ca' d'Oro, the richest example of a mature Gothic palace in Venice, the city was the wealthiest state in Europe, ruling not just the waves but also important mainland territory such as the cities of Padua, Verona, Vicenza and Bergamo. During this period Venice, and in particular the Grand Canal, was a giant building site. Palaces were enlarged, façades added, new buildings constructed, and the city became a showcase for the merchants and noblemen who had contributed to, and benefited from, Venice's golden age.

The original Veneto-Byzantine palace here, the Ca' Zeno, was, like the current palace, built to an asymmetrical plan. Contarini reused most of the piles, and appropriated ancient capitals from the ground floor (still visible from the courtyard) and 13th-century decorative features. But it is the flamboyant Gothic façade, the work of two teams of master masons – one Milanese led by Matteo Raverti, and the other led by Venetians Giovanni and Bartolomeo Bon – that still strikes awe in the hearts and minds of visitors. Originally, the 23,000 sheets of gold leaf added by the French painter Jean Charlier (called Zuane da Franza in Venice) and the costly vermilion and ultramarine decoration (all now worn away) reinforced the Ca' d'Oro's impact, and linked this private house to state buildings with exotic decoration such as the gilded window of the Maggior Consiglio in the Palazzo Ducale and San Marco itself.

The façade is a balance of solid stone and voids which, along with the open loggias, give an airy, celebratory feel to the building. The screens to the upper loggia, highly reminiscent of the tracery work of the Palazzo Ducale, were done by Raverti, while the Bon workshop was responsible for most of the rest, including the crenellation – another reference to the Palazzo Ducale – and the smaller windows. Surfaces are clad completely with marble, a very expensive material even then, and Istrian stone.

Matteo Raverti and Giovanni and Bartolomeo Bon 1420–34

CA' D'ORO

The restored courtyard has a strong Moorish influence, with its stunning rustic mosaic floor, staircase, coffered ceiling, ancient columns with wooden spreading capitals, and red marble wellhead by Bartolomeo Bon. The restoration of this courtyard was the painstaking work of the collector Giorgio Franchetti, who bought the palace in 1894 and in 1916 gave it to the state. The restoration was necessary because it had been completely taken apart by its previous owner, the ballet dancer Maria Taglioni. Ruskin had witnessed this, and remembers, while drawing the palace, 'trying to work while one sees the cursed plasterers hauling up beams & dashing in the old walls & shattering the mouldings ...'.

The interior, now modernised, was first opened to the public in 1927 and houses some fine Venetian sculpture – including Tullio Lombardo's famous *Double Portrait*. In 1972 Carlo Scarpa provided gallery fittings in his signature materials of wood, metal and stone, including sleek benching, with interlocking planks and brass detail, crisp display cabinets and iron skirting boards around the first-floor loggia – from which there's a perfect view of the Grand Canal.

LOCATION Grand Canal. Side access from the Calle Ca' d'Oro
VAPORETTO Ca' d'Oro, or *traghetto* to Campo Santa Sofia from the Peschiera
ACCESS open daily, 8.15–19.15, but note that the courtyard is occasionally closed for functions
VIEWPOINT from the Pescheria on the opposite bank of the Grand Canal

Matteo Raverti and Giovanni and Bartolomeo Bon 1420–34

MADONNA DELL'ORTO

Founded in the mid 14th century by the Umiliati order, the present church was rebuilt in the 15th century and rededicated to a statue of the Madonna which, while languishing in the adjacent vegetable patch (*orto*), had taken on miraculous healing powers. The scale and proportions of the brickwork façade are particularly satisfying, while the balance of stonework detailing lightens and enlivens the whole. The raking lines of apostles are unique in Venice and, it has been speculated, may derive from similar detailing on the cathedral at Parma, home of the original architect – Fra Tiberio. The main portal, by Bartolomeo Bon, responsible for such pure Gothic works as the Porta della Carta at the Palazzo Ducale, was created in the early 1460s but is a stylistic hybrid incorporating both Gothic and Renaissance forms. The Gothic ogee arch supporting the statue of St Christopher – to whom the original church had been dedicated – encloses a purely Renaissance element reminiscent of Codussi's work at San Michele in Isola almost 20 years later. Since it is known that the portal was not in fact installed until 1483, it is plausible that the Renaissance form was a late addition to update an otherwise already outdated style.

The internal feel is of lightness with slender oriental marble columns supporting a simple trussed wooden ceiling. This was Tintoretto's parish church and for many visitors the chief attractions are his two huge works of 1546 – the *Last Judgement* and the *Golden Calf* – flanking the altar.

CANNAREGIO

LOCATION Campo Madonna dell'Orto
VAPORETTO Madonna dell'Orto
ACCESS open Monday to Saturday, 10.00–17.30; Sunday and holidays, 13.00–17.30

Bartolomeo Bon 14th–15th centuries

SANT'ALVISE

Commissioned in the 1380s by Antonia Venier (daughter of the doge), after Sant'Alvise appeared to her in a vision, this industrial-looking Gothic church with a polygonal apse is at first sight disapppointing. Its exterior is much remodelled and its interior inauspicious. It is, however, a living example of a religious foundation, with its monastery, cloisters and herb garden still intact. The current sisterhood has been established here for 150 years.

The canalside façade sports a 15th-century Tuscan figure of Sant'Alvise, while the façade overlooking the campo is enlivened by tall windows with round arches and Gothic lights, and a now-unused public pulpit. Inside are eight little paintings, called by Ruskin 'baby Carpaccios', although actually by another pupil of Lazzaro Bastiani. Characteristic of Augustinian churches, and one of the first examples in Venice, is the *barco*, or nuns' gallery, across the west end of the nave and down the south side leading to the convent. The nuns would enter and follow mass without being seen. Today, they have their own conventual chapel.

The two sets of cloisters are reached through the convent nursery school. The first is green and shady, the wide brick arches springing from stone-capitalled columns, the whole overlooked by a bell tower topped with a brick cone. The second, now glazed in, is a miscellany of styles. Round and pointed arches, and windows, pillars and capitals from different centuries, cluster around a beautiful 14th-century raised wellhead.

LOCATION Campo di Sant' Alvise
VAPORETTO Sant' Alvise
ACCESS open Monday to Saturday, 10.00–17.30; Sunday, 15.00–17.00. To see the cloister, knock on the door of the nursery school (in the convent building adjacent to main façade) and ask to look round (weekday mornings)

CANNAREGIO

14th–15th centuries

PALAZZO MASTELLI AND THE CAMPO DEI MORI

Moorish sculptures and architectural decoration abound in Venice – a result of trade and the crusades. The most distinctive motif is perhaps the moulding of little rectangular blocks alternating on either side of a central line termed 'Venetian Dentil' – and indeed they are like teeth. Examples can be seen all over the city, including around the arched windows of the Ca' Loredan and the doorway of San Giacometto.

As well as using Moorish architectural decoration, the Venetians also included Eastern artefacts and sculptures in their buildings. The camel was a favourite image, seen here as a bas-relief built into the façade of the Gothic Palazzo Mastelli or 'del Cammello', remodelled rather unsatisfactorily in the 15th century. The camel, which James Morris thinks has an 'unkind snigger', is led by a Moor whose head is turned quizzically upwards.

Around the nearby Campo dei Mori are sculptures of four figures with turbans, again built into the walls of houses. Apart from the corner figure of the porter, now sporting a metal nose, these are unconvincing, seemingly pieced together from different statues. Accounts of their origin vary: they could represent members of the Mastelli family, originally spice merchants from Morea in Greece, or they may publicise the brothers' mercantile activities, or possibly relate to the Moro family, whose family insignia can be found within the Palazzo Mastelli. In any event, this is an interesting spot.

LOCATION Campo dei Mori, near Tintoretto's house
VAPORETTO Madonna dell'Orto
ACCESS not usually open to the public
VIEWPOINT from the Fondamenta
Gasparo Contarini

15th century

PALAZZO GIOVANELLI

Situated on a *rio* between the Maddalena and the Ca' d'Oro, the Palazzo Giovanelli appears to be a perfect late-15th-century Gothic palace. And so it is, except that the interior was restructured in the mid-nineteenth century by Giovanni Battista Meduna who had, with his brother Tommaso, rebuilt the Fenice opera house after the 1837 fire. The work was commissioned by Andrea Giovanelli, whose family palazzo this was, to provide a suitable environment for delegates of the ninth congress of Italian scientists. Giovanelli was chairman of the congress. Much of the new interior complemented the original architecture, including a beautiful Gothic spiral staircase, but there is also an elaborately gilded Renaissance-style meeting room which housed the delegates.

A 19th-century print of the exterior shows that the brickwork was originally patterned. No sign of this decoration survives today, but the symmetrical façade (earlier Gothic palaces, for example, the Ca' d'Oro, were assymetrical), the lower floor and portal separated by a cornice from the upper storeys, combines strength and stability with a lightness of touch. The seven-light, florid Gothic *piano-nobile* windows and nine simpler windows above are flanked by single windows and matching corner lights on both levels.

On the other side of, and set back from the *rio* is a tall, thin, made-to-measure, predominantly Gothic-revival palazzetto, with many late-Gothic features and marble decoration drawn from Venice's golden age. It is so neatly tucked into the cityscape that the only entrance appears to be the water gate.

LOCATION Rio Noale, Strada Nuova, Cannaregio
VAPORETTO San Marcuola/Ca' d'Oro
ACCESS not generally open to the public

Giovanni Battista Meduna (interior) 15th century, rebuilt 1847–48

SAN GIOBBE

Job (Giobbe) suffered horribly from boils and sores, and was thus a useful saint to plague-ridden Venetians. Like Moses (San Moisè) he was an Old Testament figure appropriated for Christianity. The restructuring of this church, funded by Doge Cristoforo Moro (perhaps the model for Shakespeare's Othello) was intended to honour the fiery preacher, San Bernadino of Siena, a guest of the Observant Franciscans here. It was begun by Gambello in 1450, but it is the work of Pietro Lombardo that entrances visitors today. Inside, he constructed the dome over the chancel, which some sources claim to be the first truly Renaissance dome in Venice (although others point out that the hemispherical shape and the position of the eight windows are typically Byzantine). Light from the windows throws into relief the carved altar by Lombardo and his assistants. Beneath is the pavement tomb of the doge and his wife, Cristina Sanudo. Outside, Lombardo carved the Renaissance portal, Florentine in feel and typical of his early work in Venice.

Other highlights include the Martini family chapel (Tuscan architect, 1471–76), with an unusual dome, decorated with della Robbia tiles; the Grimani chapel (1529), a much simpler, but very fine, design; and the Cozzi choir stalls. Guarding the tomb of the French ambassador, René d'Argenson, by Claude Perrault (1651) are, according to James Morris, 'the ugliest pair of lions in Venice'.

To the right of the church are its cloisters. The best view of the Gothic campanile is from the other side of the Cannaregio Canal.

LOCATION Campo San Giobbe, near the Ponte dei Tre Archi over the Cannaregio Canal
VAPORETTO Ponte dei Tre Archi
ACCESS open Monday to Saturday, 10.00–12.00, 16.00–18.00

Antonio Gambello/Pietro Lombardo 1450–93

CAPPELLA CORNARO (OR CORNER), SANTI APOSTOLI

The façade of Santi Apostoli, one of the oldest churches in Venice, is a forlorn and neglected affair. Architecturally a mish-mash – the result of the improvements endured since its foundation in the 7th century by St Magnus – the church is rescued gloriously by two features: the Renaissance Corner family chapel, probably by Pietro Lombardo, and the late-17th-/early-18th-century campanile by Andrea Tirali.

Built when Venetian architecture was in transition between Gothic and Renaissance, this chapel is one of three – see also the Martini chapel at San Giobbe and the Gussoni at San Lio – where private patrons (in this case Zorzi Corner, brother of Caterina, Queen of Cyprus) embraced the principles of Renaissance design. Built in the form of a domed temple, it faces the Campo dei Santi Apostoli, where it nestles, beautifully proportioned, among strongly coloured domestic buildings, its hemispherical dome echoing the shape of the apse and the composition balanced by the two circular oculi. Internally, four fluted Corinthian columns support the innovative strongly moulded cornice and pendentive arches to the roof. This is a complete miniature piece of restrained classical architecture, which can be compared and contrasted with the far more ornate work by Lombardo at San Lio. The campanile is 17th century, but Tirali's tambour – a concoction in pink with Istrian stone detailing setting off an octagonal tower and delicate onion dome – was added in the early 18th century.

LOCATION Campo Santi Apostoli
VAPORETTO Ca' d'Oro. Good view of the campanile from the Pescheria area (cross on Traghetto Santa Sofia)
ACCESS open daily, 7.30–11.30 and 15.00–19.00

Pietro Lombardo 1480s/Andrea Tirali (tambour) 17th century

SANTA MARIA DEI MIRACOLI

Pietro Lombardo's Renaissance masterpiece on this restricted site is a perfect little box of goodies, all the more delightful because it is of a piece, the sculptural decoration fully integrated with the architectural form of the building. Despite recent restoration, it has remained more-or-less unaltered since it was completed. Even Ruskin, vitriolic critic of Renaissance buildings, conceded its beauty.

Built on the site of a St Clare convent to house the early-15th-century miraculous picture of the Virgin by Niccolò di Pietro, now on the high altar, the church is expensively decorated with inlaid marble and porphyry slabs and discs. Unusually for Venice, all four sides of the church can be seen. One façade overlooks a canal and the pinky-yellow of the marble is caught lightly in a watery reflection, enhancing the faded and crumbling terracotta houses on the other side.

The façade has many references to classical forms, including the two superimposed orders, and pilasters and friezes framing the walls. The front façade, looking over the Corte dei Miracoli, has a semicircular gable indicating the barrel vault inside. Until the mid 19th century a nuns' walkway linked the choir of the church with the convent nearby.

Inside, all is focused on the raised chancel, with its delicate balustrade and altar screen decorated by Tullio Lombardo. Natural light floods down on to the altar from the high dome of light stone decorated with small gold stars. No wonder this is a favourite wedding venue.

LOCATION Corte dei Miracoli off Campo Santa Maria Nova
VAPORETTO Rialto
ACCESS open Monday to Saturday, 10.00–17.00; Sunday, 13.00–17.00

Pietro and Tullio Lombardo 1481–89 (restored 1997)

SAN GIOVANNI CRISOSTOMO

If this gem of a Renaissance church, with its three-part façade, crowning lunette, and curvilinear shapes, reminds you of San Zaccharia and San Michele in Isola, it is because all three churches were designed by Mauro Codussi. This was his last work, San Michele his first. Although similarly built according to the Platonic ideal that beauty was represented though simple geometric forms, the church of San Giovanni Crisostomo (named after a 5th-century patriarch of Constantinople) was constructed in poorer materials than San Michele. There is no gleaming Istrian stone here, just limestone and reddish plaster, indicative of a poor parish. Crammed into a site that crowds the tiny campo, the total effect is unusual, but friendly and welcoming.

Inside, the plan is a compact Greek cross with a dome over the axis, delineated by four columns, and small projecting apses. In the 17th century, the original barrel vault of the choir was replaced by a flat roof to accommodate new windows on the upper walls, rather spoiling Codussi's design. The condom-shaped light fittings are unfortunate, but compensated for by the Bellini altarpiece and a bas-relief of the Coronation of the Virgin by Tullio Lombardo (north side, second altar).

The original campanile, demolished in 1532, can be seen in Carpaccio's painting, *The Miracle of the Holy Cross at the Rialto Bridge* (in the Accademia gallery). The base of the present bell tower is interestingly decorated with patterns in red plaster.

LOCATION Salizzada San Giovanni Crisostomo
VAPORETTO Rialto
ACCESS open Monday to Saturday, 10.00–18.30; Sunday, 11.30–18.30

Mauro Codussi 1497–1504

PALAZZO LOREDAN-VENDRAMIN-CALERGI

With this palace, Codussi mastered the integration of the traditional Venetian plan within a classically consistent façade. The central three windows, divided by single Corinthian columns, define the major reception spaces, while single windows to either side, framed by a double order of columns, reflect the ancillary accommodation. This was patrician design on the grandest scale seen to date; so much so that the client – Andrea Loredan – sought to counter criticisms of self-aggrandisment with the canal-side inscription 'Non Nobis Dne/Non Nobis' (not for us Lord, not for us). In its design can be seen the confident development of Codussi's Palazzo Lando-Corner-Spinelli. Strong horizontal banding now works with the verticals to produce a organising framework for the overall design which gives the appearance of uniform height floors. This has been achieved by a series of subtle design devices – for example, the true height of the first floor is visually reduced through raising column bases to the level of the balustrading, while the second floor appears to gain height by omitting a balustrade and basing the columns on the first-floor entablature. If compared with, for instance, the Ca' d'Oro, the stylistic developments of the previous century are now clear – asymmetry and eclecticism rooted in the Gothic style have given way to symmetry, uniformity and classicism. Highly admired from the time of its construction, the writer Francesco Sansovino declared it 'among the most important of all the palaces on the Grand Canal ... the front all sheathed in Greek marble'.

LOCATION Grand Canal/Campiello Vendramin (Cannaregio)

VAPORETTO San Marcuola

ACCESS restricted public access (used as Venice's casino during winter months)

VIEWPOINT Deposito del Megio (Santa Croce)

Mauro Codussi 1502–09

THE GHETTO

For a completely different, and sobering, Venetian experience, make for the Jewish Ghetto. The apartment buildings, built high to accommodate an expanding community, tower over Venice's housing stock and today confer a peaceful atmosphere, particularly on the Campo Ghetto Nuovo. In the past, however, they formed a prison wall. The story of the Venetian Jews is similar to their story elsewhere – periods of toleration alternating with years of persecution, restrictions, humiliations. The Ghetto architecture is indicative of that story.

Jews escaping persecution started to arrive in Venice possibly as early as the 11th century. They came from the East (Levantine Jews), from Spain and Portugal (Ponentini) and from Germany and Italy (Ashkenazi). Excluded in 1298, they were allowed back after a 1516 decree granted them the right to work (with restrictions) and worship in the city, but also enclosed them in the Ghetto Nuovo, an island with only two access points and policed at night by sentries the Jews had to pay for themselves. The word 'ghetto', now synonymous with any area of ethnic or religious isolation, is a mispronunciation by Ashkenazi Jews of '*geto*' (soft 'g') from *getare*, 'to smelt'. The metal foundries here relocated to the Arsenale in the early 15th century. Confusingly, the Ghetto Nuovo was the first Jewish area: in 1541 the population spilled into the Ghetto Vecchio. The Ghetto Nuovissimo was added in 1633 when the population reached around 5000.

The tenement apartments are cramped, with very low ceilings, but they would often house two families each. Now only five Jewish families live in the Ghetto – the rest of the 450-strong community lives elsewhere, liberated in 1797 by Napoleon.

SYNAGOGUES

There are five main synagogues or '*schole*'. The Tedesca (the oldest, built in 1528, and closed at present), Canton (1553, 'canton' is Venetian for 'corner') and Italian (1575) were

15th–17th centuries

THE GHETTO

built into existing buildings in the Ghetto Nuovo, and only the Canton, with its clapboarding and leaded-light lantern, is immediately obvious from the outside. All, however, are marked by five arched windows representing the first five books of the Bible. These three synagogues were inconspicuous, partly owing to financial restraints, partly because of fear of persecution. They are located on upper storeys because a liturgical requirement specified that no accommodation should be built above them.

The Canton synagogue, a popular wedding venue, is richly decorated, with elaborately carved, twisted wooden columns and wooden panels. Such intricate work made up for the lack of gold and marble which were prohibited to this Jewish group. Gilt and *marmorino* were used to great effect instead. There's a women's gallery on one side.

The Campiello delle Scuole at the end of the Ghetto Vecchio houses the synagogues of the Levantine and Spanish Jews, decidedly more lavish in their decoration. These are the only two in regular use. The Levantine façade (1538, winter use), by pupils of Longhena's, has the most distinct architectural form. Inside, the exquisite carved woodwork, painted black by the Austrians, is by Andrea Brustolon, a pupil of Bernini. The Spagnola (1584, though established earlier, summer use) has an interior rebuilt by Longhena in 1655 and an attractive women's gallery (no longer used).

LOCATION Campo Ghetto Nuovo/Ghetto Vecchio
VAPORETTO Ponte delle Guglie
ACCESS guided tours of three synagogues leave the museum every hour from 10.30–17.30, June to September, or until 15.30, October to May, excluding Jewish holidays

Baldassare Longhena and his school 1516–1633 (Levantine and Spagnola synagogues)

FARMACIA F PONTI

There are several old pharmacies in Venice, but this one, used daily for business until the late 1990s and then restored to its full glory, has a really stunning interior. From the street you can see in through the windows, but ask in the modern pharmacy next door to be allowed in through the low wrought-iron gate.

The rich wood carving of the walls, the medical cabinets and the counter all date from the end of the 17th century. The style is heavy baroque, complete with broken pediments and carved statues and reliefs, which seem completely suited to the serious and ponderous task of dispensing medicines. The blue and white medicine bottles, hinged benches and all other cabinet fittings are also part of the original fit-out.

The pharmacy is well worth a stop while investigating this area or on your way to or from the train station. Devotees can also visit the still-functioning Farmacia Pisanello in Campo San Polo, opposite the church, which contains some fine terracotta sculptures set against gold mosaic backgrounds.

CANNAREGIO

LOCATION Strada Nova, Cannaregio
VAPORETTO San Marcuola or Ca' d'Oro
ACCESS open Monday to Saturday, 8.30–13.00, 15.30–19.00

17th-century interior

PALAZZO LABIA

This final great palace of the late-baroque style has, unusually, three decorative façades – two 17th-century façades on the Cannaregio Canal and turning to face the Grand Canal, and an 18th-century example, thought to be by Tremignon, fronting Campo San Geremia.

The Labia merchants had arrived in Venice in the mid 16th century. They quickly, through their dealings in military supplies, became so wealthy that in 1646, through a huge donation to the by-then-impoverished Republic, they were able to buy entry to the Venetian aristocracy. This palace was immediately commissioned to reflect their new-found status. The 17th-century façades, epitomising late baroque and reminiscent of Longhena's work at Ca' Pesaro, are embellished with grotesque masks and the massive eagle of the Labia coat of arms. Tremignon's façade to the palace's subsequent enlargement, while clearly similar, has a restraint that anticipates the rejection of baroque excess in favour of a calmer neoclassicism later seen at Palazzo Grassi. The palace contains Tiepolo's Venetian masterpiece – a series of frescoes portraying the story of Anthony and Cleopatra, decorating a magnificent double-storey ballroom carved out of the centre of the building. It has been suggested that such an important work symbolically proclaimed Venice, no longer a major trading nation, to be the new art capital of Europe.

At the Republic's fall the family departed, the palace being repeatedly sold on. Reaching its nadir as low-rent apartment housing (the ballroom became a laundry room), it was finally restored in the 1970s by RAI, whose regional headquarters it now houses.

CANNAREGIO

LOCATION Campo San Geremia/Fondamenta Labia
VAPORETTO Ferrovia
ACCESS by appointment with RAI, tel 041 5242812, fax 041 5240675

Andrea Cominelli/Alessandro Tremignon 1685, extended 1720

GESUITI CHURCH
SANTA MARIA ASSUNTA

In 1657, the Jesuits bought the church of the Crociferi (an order suppressed in 1656 for moral turpitude), located in an area devoted to the guilds of tailors, weavers and coopers (see the insignia on local houses). Funded by the Manin family, who are buried here, reconstruction started in 1713. Domenico Rossi, Giuseppe Sardi's nephew, was briefed on the order's requirements and collaborated with other architects and sculptors to come up with a specially adapted Latin-cross plan. The form, however, is overshadowed by the unique 18th-century interior, reminiscent of a magnificent ballroom – theatrical, yes, spiritual, no.

The walls are almost entirely covered in green-grey marble inlay decoration, mimicking a rich tapestry. Ditto the realistically draped pulpit. Indeed, the only undecorated surfaces are the flat pilasters, the arches to the chapels and the cornices. Pozzo's high altar contains a majolica *baldacchino*, lit in blue from underneath and resembling a Disneyworld grotto. Also in the church are the Lezze monument attributed to Sansovino and paintings by Titian, Palma the Younger and Tintoretto.

The façade, often attributed to Fattoretto, is richly decorated with huge Corinthian columns, an elaborate architrave, statues of the apostles and, above the doorway, the Manin coat-of-arms. The clothes of the angels on the roofline seem to blow in the wind.

For a history of the Crociferi, visit the Oratorio diagonally opposite the church, which contains an impressive cycle of narrative paintings by Palma the Younger.

CANNAREGIO

LOCATION Campo dei Gesuiti, off Fondamenta Nuove

VAPORETTO Fondamenta Nuove

ACCESS Gesuiti open daily, 10.00–12.00, 17.00–19.00; Oratorio open April to October, daily, 10.00–13.30

Domenico Rossi (with G del Pozzo, G Torretto, A Stazio, G B Fattoretto) c 1713–30

SANTA MARIA MADDALENA
LA MADDALENA

La Maddalena is open only rarely, but don't miss visiting the delightful quiet campo on the curve of a canal, a setting that shows off this cylindrical church to perfection.

Temanza, a leading neoclassical scholar, based his projects on classical geometric rules – to a large extent a backlash against baroque excess. He was proud of this church where, he said, 'the external parts correspond exactly to the interior and the proportions are musical'. The architect Giorgio Massari, however, felt it was a pagan design that failed to meet the needs of religious ceremonies.

La Maddalena makes reference to the Pantheon in Rome as well as to Temanza's earlier work, the oratory of Santa Margherita in Padua. It is faced in wonderful smooth marble, with a façade in the form of a pronaos with Ionic columns and capitals.

The interior hexagonal plan includes four symmetrical chapels within semicircular arches. The church is lit by a tiny cupola. The one exception to classical regularity is the apse, a separate space that echoes Palladio's church designs.

Temanza died in 1789 and the project was completed by his student, Giannantonio Selva, who later designed the Fenice opera house (currently being restored after the 1997 fire). The campo, with an attractive wellhead, is overlooked on the west by picturesque 13th- and 14th-century houses (Nos. 2111, 2112, 2114 and 2115), delighting the eye with their different shapes, heights and colours, and supporting an army of chimneys. The pinky-cream building with a Gothic lunette adjoining La Maddalena is the Palazzo Magno.

LOCATION Campo della Maddalena

VAPORETTO San Marcuola

ACCESS open variable hours – Christmas and some feast days only

Tommaso Temanza / Gianantonio Selva c 1763–89

MACELLO
CENTRAL ABBATOIR

Constructed during the period of Austrian occupation, the Macello consolidated what had hitherto been a motley collection of housing and workshops fronting the Lagoon. Its understated grandeur in the neoclassical style was intended to work in tandem with the contemporary railway bridge to the mainland, to present a very different, rationally ordered face to the visitor to Venice arriving by this radically new means. Behind the restrained main façades a series of finely detailed courtyards open off the central alleyway. The building complex was still in use during the 1960s – James Morris recounting how cattle would be driven through the Alley of Butchers from the railway twice a week. Then, in 1964, a masterplan commissioned from Le Corbusier laid out proposals for the site's redevelopment as the new city hospital. However, in the face of opposition to the abbatoir's demolition (including, it is said, from Le Corbusier himself), the plans were abandoned.

No longer functioning as an abbatoir, the site has recently been restored to form part of the University Ca' Foscari. Relatively minimal architectural intervention has created a series of offices and lecture halls to breathe fresh life into this striking complex of buildings.

CANNAREGIO

LOCATION Fondamenta di San Giobbe
VAPORETTO Tre Archi
ACCESS during academic semesters

Giuseppe Salvadori 1841–43; EDIL Venezia (restoration and conversion)

FERROVIA
RAILWAY STATION

Although unloved by most, no architectural guide to Venice could ignore the railway station – ultimate symbol of Venice's fall to the advance of the mainland and, architecturally, a unique anachronism on the Grand Canal. It was the railway link which, in 1846, was to end Venice's physical separation from the mainland, and enable the occupying Austrian forces to garrison the island efficiently. Construction of its terminus station involved wholesale demolition of the Church of Santa Lucia and the buildings leading up to the Scalzi church. Architecturally it was considered poor and so in 1934 a competition was held for its replacement. There was no clear winner so that, combined with the subsequent disruption caused by the Second World War, today's building was not constructed until the 1950s. Its exaggerated horizontal style ensures no connection with the Venetian architectural context and it is still the cuckoo in the nest that it always has been, both architecturally and symbolically.

The grand staircase entrance now seems inappropriate: it restricts access and provides a further barrier through its use as impromptu seating. The unresolved piazza fronting the Grand Canal is another problem area. There is, however, a touch of almost desperate humour in the glazed entrance canopy, decorated as it is with images of fish.

CANNAREGIO

LOCATION Fondamenta Santa Lucia
VAPORETTO Ferrovia (Stazione)
ACCESS open during commercial hours

Paolo Perilli with the State Railway Technical Office 1952–55

HOUSING AT SAN GIOBBE

Following one of the *calle* running back from the Fondamenta Savorgnan leads you into an extensive area of 1980s public housing which seeks to reinterpret the traditional Venetian urban grain in a contemporary style. This area had previously been given over to industrial use, and memories of such architecture can be found at the margins of the development. In laying out the complex the architect has formed a hierarchy of public, semi-public and private open spaces, creating a familiar Venetian environment. For instance, in one 'street', terraces face each other across a central garden that takes the place of canal water, and in the central square a modern wellhead mimics tradition. At ground level on the main streets are shop units. Behind and above, housing units are stacked into four-storey terraces with ground- and first-floor access. Their pink rendered forms contain many uniquely Venetian architectural elements, such as the open rooftop *altana*, white stone detailing for cornice, plinth and door surrounds, and elaborate chimneys.

Early reviews of the scheme praised its achievements in recreating a lively community in the Venetian tradition. Ten years later, however, many of the commercial units have closed, the stripped-back detailing of some of its buildings is looking tired and much of its public planting is neglected – all-too-frequent evidence of the true complexity of knitting an area back into a city's socio-economic life. The whole can be interestingly compared with Gino Valle's work at IACP on Giudecca.

CANNAREGIO

LOCATION Campiello Pesaro
VAPORETTO Ponte delle Guglie/Ponte dei Scalzi

Vittorio Gregotti and assistants 1984–94

HOUSING AT SACCA DI SAN GIROLAMO

The point at which the Cannaregio Canal enters the Lagoon is framed by this residential complex of 47 dwellings and the recently restored 19th-century Macello. It is an important frontage visible from the mainland and the connecting bridge. Perhaps the best vantage point to first appreciate the architect's intentions in balancing the scale and design elements of the adjoining Macello is from the passing *vaporetto* route. From here the housing's two-storey Lagoon frontage of pink render with green-shuttered windows can be seen to incorporate elements of a grander scale – residual stone columns and a rhythm of arched openings. Behind this elevation the development rises in a wedge to four storeys, with roofs incorporating a forest of traditionally shaped funnel chimneys. On land, the complex is entered through a rather theatrical arch incorporating a suspended oculus. The housing is laid out around a main street and series of courts, opening up to the Lagoon frontage. Along the water's edge boat moorings reinforce the essential relationship between Venetian citizens and the water.

Detailing is simple but robust with stone dressings to windows and doors. The elegant proportions of the tall shuttered windows and the introduction of porthole windows as a key design element that echo the shape of the entrance arch are visually satisfying. The whole maintains a feeling of intimacy which, given its good state of repair, seems clearly appreciated by those who live there.

CANNAREGIO

LOCATION Fondamenta di Cannaregio
VAPORETTO Tre Archi

Franco Bortoluzzi and the City Urban Planning Office 1987–90

CASTELLO

ARSENALE

By the 14th century, Venice's shipyard, the Arsenale (in Arabic, *d'arsina* means 'place of industry') was already a tourist attraction (Dante was bowled over by it), rivalling the Palazzo Ducale as the symbol of Venetian state power, and competing with the naval bases at Pisa and Genoa for strategic importance. It continued to grow, reaching its zenith in the latter half of the 16th century. Here the great Venetian fleet was constructed using production-line techniques that predated Britain's industrial revolution by 400 years. It has been recorded how, in 1574 , the newly crowned Henri III of France was taken one morning to see the keel of a ship being laid, returning later in the day to see the same ship, fully equipped, being launched. As a classically styled, pre-modern industrial complex, the buildings making up the Arsenale are unrivalled. The *arsenalotti* who worked here and lived in the surrounding area had special privileges and an important role in city life.

Unfortunately, the Arsenale, which lies behind high brick walls with traditional Venetian crenellations, is currently a military zone and visitors can no longer take *vaporetto* No. 5 through the area. Most tourists get no further than the land gate. This was built in 1460 and is one of the first examples of Roman-influenced Renaissance architecture in Venice. It is attributed to Antonio Gambello, the Republic's military architect, who was motivated by the writings of the contemporary classical scholar, Doge Pasquale Malipiero. The design of the triumphal arch is taken from the ancient Roman arch at Pola in Istria. The winged victories above the arch and the figure of Santa Giustina were added after the victory of Lepanto in 1570. (The battle took place on the saint's feast day.) A rather fierce winged lion of Venice tops the arch under a triangular pediment and guards the book bearing the legend *Pax Tibe Marce* (see Introduction, page 0.7). The lions flanking the land gate were brought here from Athens by Francesco Morosini in the late 17th

Antonio Gambello, Jacopo Sansovino, Antonio da Ponte, Michele Sanmicheli 1104–1879

ARSENALE

century, while the lion on the far right, with a newly modelled head, is 6th-century and comes from Delos.

Beyond the land gate, however, lies the heart of the Arsenale: the great shipbuilding sheds, Sanmicheli's 16th-century building that housed the Bucintoro (the doge's barge), da Ponte's *corderia* (the ropeworks), the awesome wet docks with fat Piranesi-like columns, attributed to Jacopo Sansovino, and the 16th-century water gate at the northern end. Also in evidence is work undertaken by the Austrians after 1814 and later 19th-century modernisation which included the building of the dry docks in 1875–79 (north-eastern corner).

The area was a naval base during both world wars but is now almost wholly unused. However, during the October 2000 Biennale, devoted to architecture, parts were used as an exhibition area and visitors could wander through the monumental *corderia* right up to the wet docks with a view of the water gate. If this becomes the norm, do everything you can to gain entrance. It's one of the greatest experiences Venice has to offer.

LOCATION at the far eastern end of Castello

VAPORETTO Arsenale

ACCESS the land gate is viewable. Serious visitors wishing to gain admission to the complex should start by enquiring at the tourist office, currently housed in the Coffee House, *sestiere* San Marco

Antonio Gambello, Jacopo Sansovino, Antonio da Ponte, Michele Sanmicheli 1104–1879

SANT'APOLLONIA CLOISTER

Escape the bustle of the Piazza San Marco and make for this beautifully restored oasis. Along with the church of Santi Filippo e Giacomo (demolished in the 18th century – only the stone doorway remains), the cloister was once part of Santa Scholastica, a Benedictine monastery. In 1472 the church and monastery came under the doge's jurisdiction, and until 1810 the *primicerio* of St Mark's, the most important priest in the Basilica, lived here. As the only surviving example of a complete Romanesque cloister in Venice, it is a gem.

The plan is rectangular, with a herringbone terracotta pavement in the central courtyard (note the Veneto-Byzantine wellhead), and a simpler pavement in the portico. The single and delicately paired columns rise from a terracotta wall and support irregular arches low enough to give the cloister an intimate feel. On the upper level are attractive five-light windows, behind which an exhibition space provides a good view over the cloister. At the far end is the entrance to the Museo Diocesiano, but a stroll around the cloister with its wooden beamed ceiling and photographs of the restoration is a better bet.

The words of the poet Gabriele d'Annunzio (1863–1938) are commemorated on a plaque by the cloister entrance. Entranced by the colour given to the stone by the light he described it as '...not white, not grey, not black, but the most mysterious colour given to stone by that great master colourist known as time'.

LOCATION Fondamenta Sant'Apollonia/Ruga Giuffa
VAPORETTO San Zaccaria
ACCESS cloister usually open, times vary. Museo Diocesano d'Arte Sacre open daily, 10.30–12.30

12th century, restored 1960s

CORTE BOTTERA

This small domestic courtyard between Santi Giovanni e Paolo and Santa Maria Formosa is a unique architectural evocation of traditional patterns of Venetian life, all but lost elsewhere in the city. It is notoriously difficult to find, being reached through a gated round-arched entrance leading off a cantilevered walkway at the point where the Ponte del Conzafelzi lands on the Fondamenta Felzi at the head of the Calle Pinelli. Through the entrance, steps descend to the Sotopòrtego Botera and lead into a scene which charts its architectural development from the 13th century. To the right, a Gothic, columned *sotopòrtego* opens on to the canal. Opposite are the vestiges of the original land-side entrance – a fine Byzantine stone arch carved with floral and animalistic decoration. Along one side a 14th-century external staircase leads to the first floor, while in the centre is a Gothic wellhead. Taken together, the two gates, the stair and the wellhead serving a small courtyard constitute the Corte Bottera – a distinctly Venetian domestic enclosure.

Over the centuries, however, there have clearly been many modifications and stylistic updates. The most extraordinary is perhaps the 19th-century window, reflecting the habitation of space previously used for storage, and blatantly cutting into one side of the Byzantine arch.

LOCATION Calle Pinelli/Fondamenta Felzi
VAPORETTO Ospedale
ACCESS public access, but gate is sometimes closed

13th–19th centuries

CAMPO BANDIERA E MORO
FORMERLY KNOWN AS CAMPO BRAGORA

At the beginning of the 9th century, even before the central Venetian islands became the seat of power for the future Republic, there were already 24 parishes; San Giovanni in Bragora was one of these. A parish's *campo* (field) is an archetypal element of the Venetian cityscape. Originally grassed, hence the name, it is the equivalent of the village green – the community's heart. In its centre is the *vera da pozzo*, or wellhead, of Istrian stone; it crowns an underground cistern for the collection, filtering and storage of rain to provide drinking water. Perched over the tiled roofs (for instance above Nos. 3610/3612) are communal *altane*, or roof terraces – private outside space in a city notoriously short of such a facility. Two buildings dominate this campo, balancing the community's secular and religious influences – the 14th-century former Palazzo Gritti-Badoer (Nos. 3608/3609) and the church of San Giovanni in Bragora. The former, constructed 1310–20, incorporates a perfect example, at first-floor level, of a Gothic five-light window. Set in a panel of marble cladding with the typical roundels founded in Veneto-Byzantine style, it is crowned with a family coat of arms and carving of a peacock – the traditional symbol of resurrection. It was home to a branch of the noble Gritti family but, by the 19th century, had been abandoned – in Ruskin's words, 'a ruin, inhabited by the lowest orders'. Today it is La Residenza hotel, with a grand first-floor reception space decorated with typically elaborate 18th-century plasterwork.

The church façade dates from 1475. Termed transitional in style, it is reminiscent of the purely Gothic form of, for example, the Frari but, in its rounded tripartite roofline, anticipates the Renaissance style of San Zaccaria. The original belltower would have been more imposing but in all probability collapsed (a potential danger to which many leaning Venetian towers testify), to be replaced by today's more modest structure. To the left of the church is its former 17th-century *scuola* building whose work in the community was

14th–20th centuries

CAMPO BANDIERA E MORO

curtailed by Napoleon (see Introduction, pages 0.11–0.14). The rest of the *campo* displays a range of Venetian architecture from the 14th–20th centuries. Nos. 3812/3814 are modest 17th-century apartment housing with shops at ground level.

Campi were, however, typically home to the community's leading families – to the left of the Gritti palazzo stands a minor 17th-century palazzo, with swirling baroque volutes to its dormer window (Nos. 3610/3612), and a second Gothic palazzo (Nos. 3626/3627). At the entrance to the *campo* from Calle del Dose is an example of early-20th-century Veneto-Byzantine revivalism (No. 3805). The decorative brickwork style with stone detailing was intended to recapture the halcyon days of the Venetian Republic, and may be seen at its most grandiose in the Nardi housing complex.

The *campo* was renamed to commemorate former residents – the brothers Bandiera and their colleague Domenico Moro – freedom fighters shot in southern Italy in 1844. Perhaps more familiar to today's visitor is Venice's feted composer, Antonio Vivaldi, originally resident in Calle del Dose, and baptised in the *campo*'s church in 1678.

LOCATION Campo Bandiera e Moro (Bragora)
VAPORETTO Arsenale
ACCESS public space

14th–20th centuries

SANTI GIOVANNI E PAOLO
SAN ZANIPOLO

Second only to Piazza San Marco in its civic grandeur, the Campo dei Santi Giovanni e Paolo, focussed on Verrocchio's spectacular late-15th-century bronze equestrian statue of Bartolomeo Colleoni, is dominated by this monumental Gothic brick church and its adjoining Scuola Grande di San Marco. This was the church of the Dominican order. The Dominican and Franciscan friars were the two great mendicant orders, arriving at Venice in the 13th century, and their surviving great churches – this and the Franciscan Frari – are closely comparable in layout and detail. Their respective designated locations on land donated by the Republic ensured both their geographical separation – to avoid their followers' competitive search for donors – and their distance from the political centre.

Bartolomeo Bon's elegant main west entrance of 1460 integrates classical details into its essentially Gothic form, balancing the strength of six Greek marble columns brought from Torcello against the delicate twisted rope of intermediate colonnettes. More sophisticated than Bon's contemporary portal at the Madonna dell' Orto, it was intended as the focus for a complete remodelling of this façade (begun but not completed). Inside, the soaring brick vaulted structure – a precarious form on the shifting ground of Venice – is stabilised by the decorated timber tie-beams. Light floods in through the delicate apse windows to an interior holding 25 doges' tombs. The series of five of these monuments, constructed by the Lombardo family in the second half of the 15th century, to Pasquale Malpiero, Nicolò Marcello, Pietro Mocenigo, Andrea Vendramin and Giovanni Mocenigo, is exceptional.

LOCATION Campo dei Santi Giovanni e Paolo
VAPORETTO Ospedale
ACCESS open daily, 7.30–12.30, 15.00–18.00

Bartolomeo Bon/Lombardo family 14th–15th centuries

SCUOLA GRANDE DI SAN MARCO

Founded in 1260, this *scuola grande*, dedicated to St Mark, became hugely influential. The first building here with contributions by Bartolomeo Bon and Antonio Rizzo, begun in 1437 and finished in the 1470s, was destroyed by fire in 1485. Pietro Lombardo and Giovanni Buora were commissioned by the Republic to rebuild it. In 1490, after he had completed the façade's lower orders and some interior work and had at least designed the side façade, Lombardo was dismissed and replaced by Codussi, who completed the façade, incorporating elaborate gables at roof level, a reference to San Marco. Lombardo's contribution, with its marble sheeting, is reminiscent of his Santa Maria dei Miracoli. Pietro's son Tullio is the most likely candidate for the perspectival bas-reliefs at ground-floor level – the two lions guarding the portal (the lunette over is by Bon), and the two scenes of St Mark healing and baptising Anianus the cobbler. The overall result is a typically Venetian grand façade. Like all *scuole grandi*, it was located next to a monastic church, in this case Santi Giovanni e Paolo.

The portal, now the land entrance to the City Hospital, leads to the lower hall or *androne* (by Lombardo and Buora), from which Codussi's innovative double staircase rises to the old chapter hall, now the library (coffered ceiling by Pietro and Biagio da Faenza). This staircase resulted in Codussi's commission for the staircase at the rival Scuola Grande di San Giovanni Evangelista. Wander through to Scamozzi's church of San Lazzaro dei Mendicanti (1601–31), now the hospital chapel.

LOCATION Campo dei Santi Giovanni e Paolo

VAPORETTO Ospedale

ACCESS ground-floor rooms open. Library open Monday to Friday, 8.30–14.00; ring doorbell at library entrance

Pietro Lombardo (with Tullio), Giovanni Buora and Mauro Codussi 1437–95

PALAZZO PRIULI OSMARIN

The Priuli Osmarin, situated well away from the Grand Canal, is sited with two water frontages and two land frontages. Its original owners, the Hungarian Priuli family, had been part of Venice's ruling patriciate since the 12th century. Recently restored and converted into private apartments, it presents a patchwork of Gothic design elements. It is thought to have originally fronted the Campo San Severo – from which its main, and imposing, land entrance still gives access – and only subsequently to have been extended to the Rio San Provolo. The latter façade holds the greatest architectural interest. In the centre a wonderfully irregular panel incorporates, at ground-floor level, a group of five-lobed early-Gothic arches – the outside openings being larger than the central three at first-floor level. Above is a second series of later mid-Gothic arches. Although neither symmetrical nor in vertical alignment, the whole is unified by its placing within a fielded panel, decorated with roundels and framed with dentillated mouldings. The decorative multi-light windows would not only have proclaimed the owner's status, but also allowed vicarious nightime views of the social privilege lying behind the façade – a cameo today recaptured by the contemporary restoration work. The corner window of the façade, like windows found at the Palazzo Mastelli, adopts a style taken directly from the Palazzo Ducale. Records show that, at the beginning of the 16th century, the façade was embellished with frescoes, now lost, by Palma the Elder.

LOCATION Campo di San Severo/Rio di San Provolo
VAPORETTO San Zaccaria
ACCESS not open to the public

15th century

SAN ZACCARIA

Next to the site of a Benedictine convent famed for its nobly-born licentious nuns, San Zaccaria is a 15th-century restructuring of a already much-altered 9th-century building. Its style is transitional, with a Renaissance flavour superimposed on a Gothic structure. The state paid for the work, justified by the close relationship between the doge and the convent – he visited San Zaccaria every Easter Monday; the nuns in turn had, in the 12th century, sacrificed their vegetable garden to the enlargement of the Piazza San Marco for Doge Sebastiano Ziani.

Antonio Gambello started work on the interior in 1456, probably completing the lower order of the façade before his death in 1481. Enter Codussi, recently lauded for his work on San Michele in Isola, who finished the job. The Istrian stone tiers of colonnades – the parts as delicate as a wedding cake, the whole as powerful as a large palace – is an exercise in *chiaroscuro*, the dark windows contrasting with the white stone. The semicircular gable and supporting side quadrants with roundel windows are Codussian trademarks. To the right is the earlier Gothic church and access to the convent.

Inside, parts of the older churches are clearly visible, but it is the choir, with its superimposed colonnades in Gothic and Renaissance styles, and the ambulatory behind it (common in northern Europe, rare in Italy, unique in Venice) that provide the real interest. Contemplate Giovanni Bellini's fine *Madonna and Four Saints* (1505), and note how the architecture in the painting is continued into its frame.

LOCATION Campo San Zaccaria
VAPORETTO San Zaccaria/San Marco
ACCESS open daily, 10.00–12.00, 16.00–18.00

Antonio Gambello, Mauro Codussi 9th century/1456–1500

SAN GIORGIO DEI GRECI AND THE SCOLETTA DI SAN NICCOLÒ

The exterior of Sante Lombardo's church gives no hint of its Greek Orthodox interior, unique in Venice. The single nave leads to an apse and two side chapels, protected by elaborate doorways, where part of the Orthodox service is conducted. The most startling feature, however, is the iconostasis, the traditional Orthodox altar screen – a wall of gold decorated with paintings by Greek artists, which show considerable Venetian influence. Also housed here is an icon of Christ the Pantocrator, rescued from Constantinople before it fell to the Turks in 1453. As a result the Venetian Greek population grew. Their artists and literati gave a boost to Italian Renaissance scholarship. In 1470, when the community had grown to 4000, the Greeks were granted permission by the religiously tolerant Venetians to hold their own services. The present church was begun 60 years later, the cupola by Gianantonio Chiona was added in 1571.

In the 1670s Longhena was asked to design the other buildings here, and it is his work that integrates the complex with Venetian architectural tradition. His recently restored Scoletta di San Niccolò, with its soaring cantilevered staircase and simple rectangular upstairs room, deeply modelled in dark wood, is a masterpiece. This and his Collegio Flangini (financed by a legacy from Tommaso Flangini, a wealthy Greek merchant and – in 1664 – a late entrant to the Venetian Republic's patriciate) were enclosed, with the church, behind a wall bordering the canal. The unstable campanile (1582–92) is by Simeone Sorella.

LOCATION on the Rio dei Greci, adjacent to bridge on Calle della Madonna
VAPORETTO San Zaccaria
ACCESS church open 9.00–13.00, 14.00–16.30, closed Sunday; Scoletta not usually open to the public, though the upper room is sometimes used for congresses

Sante Lombardo, Baldassare Longhena, Simone Sorella (campanile) 1530–61

SAN FRANCESCO DELLA VIGNA

Turn into the Campo della Confraternità and Palladio's façade, paid for by Giovanni Grimani in the 1560s, looms into view – one bright white, soaring temple breaking through a wider, lower one. With an unusually tall doorway and fine bronze statues of Moses and St Paul by Tiziano Aspetti, it is a powerful gateway to Sansovino's simple interior.

According to Venetian tradition, it was here that an angel told St Mark that the Lagoon was to be his resting place. The original medieval church was built by the Observant Franciscans on land that once supported a vineyard. In 1534, Doge Andrea Gritti instructed Sansovino to transform the interior into one of the earliest Venetian Renaissance works. A year later the humanist friar Francesco Zorzi revised the interior plan to fit a harmonious, neo-Platonic system based on multiples of the number three. He also stipulated that the chapels should be vaulted and the nave coffered for better accoustics. This roof was never constructed, and the existing false vault was added in 1630.

The interior plan is a Latin cross, with a wide nave and raised side chapels. Two of these have been restored recently: the Grimani chapel (first chapel, north transept), with bronze statues of Justice and Temperance by Tiziano Aspetti (1592), and the fine Giustiniani chapel on the left of the south transept which contains a 15th-century bas-relief of the life of Christ by Pietro Lombardo and reliefs of four evangelists by his son, Tullio.

The two 14th-century cloisters are delightful. The campanile, one of the tallest in the city, by Bernardo Ongarin, was built in the 1570s.

LOCATION Campo della Confraternità, north-eastern Castello
VAPORETTO Celestia
ACCESS open daily, 8.00–12.20, 15.00–19.00

Jacopo Sansovino/Andrea Palladio/Pietro Lombardo 1530–72

CA' DI DIO

Sansovino, architect of five Venetian churches, the grand palaces of the Dolfin-Manin and the Corner della Ca' Grande, as well as the Marciana Library, could also turn his hand with enthusiasm to more lowly domestic architecture. These polarised styles existed side-by-side in Venice, enriching the architectural vocabulary of the city. Sansovino's own house (1552) on Calle del Magazen, opposite the church of San Trovaso in Dorsoduro, is elegant, but simple and modest, and the same is certainly true of the Ca' di Dio.

The Ca' di Dio was originally designed (possibly in the 13th century) to house pilgrims outward bound for the Holy Land, but from the 14th century it became an oratory and an insitution housing poor women. Sansovino redesigned it with plain façades, almost factory-like in appearance, lifted by a simple first-floor *serliana* overlooking the Lagoon, a row of huge, chunky chimneys along the Rio di Dio and the warmth of its terra-cotta-coloured rendering. (The upper-floor *serliana* window is not part of Sansovino's design, but was added during the 1970s' restoration) Yet the building, like his other work in the vernacular style considered by the Republic as suitable for less central areas of the city, is dignified and impressive, not cold and austere. It is an awe-inspiring sight for walkers along the Riva di Ca' di Dio.

LOCATION Castello, Riva di Ca' di Dio, just by the Arsenale *vaporetto* stop
VAPORETTO Arsenale
ACCESS not open to the public

Jacopo Sansovino 1545–70

SCUOLA DI SAN GIORGIO DEGLI SCHIAVONI

The cycle of Carpaccio paintings in this *scuola piccola* – established in 1451 for the Schiavoni (Slavs), natives of Dalmatia, and built at the end of the 15th century – is a fine example of the commissioning power of the smaller confraternities (see Introduction, page 0.11). This is one of the few buildings in Venice where you can appreciate the paintings intended for its walls *in situ*.

The *scuola* (façade 1551 by Pietro da Salò) has two main rooms, one above the other – the usual *scuola* arrangement – and a sacristy. The lower room ('no bigger than your garage', says James Morris) contains the Carpaccios, completed between 1502 and 1507 for the upper floor. In 1565 this upstairs room was altered, and by 1586 the paintings had migrated downstairs – and cut to fit!

Like much of Carpaccio's work, this series has an architectural quality. In *St George Fighting the Dragon*, the gateway to the city of Silena is reminiscent of the Bab al-Futauh, Cairo. St Cyriacus in Ancona was the inspiration for the church on the hill above the princess. Different views of the same city feature in *The Triumph of St George* and *St George Baptising the Pagans*. The other pictures show scenes from the life of Christ, St Jerome, St Tryphon, and *The Vision of Saint Augustine*, who sees the spirit of St Jerome passing by his window. St George, St Tryphon and St Jerome are all Dalmatian saints.

The upper room has a gilded 17th-century ceiling, with paintings probably by Andrea Vicentino. Unusually, the *scuola* was spared by Napoleon. (See Introduction, page 0.17.)

LOCATION off the Calle dei Furlani

VAPORETTO San Zaccaria

ACCESS open Tuesday to Saturday, 10.00–12.30, 15.00–18.00; Sunday, 10.00–12.30

Pietro da Salò 1551–58

SAN MARTINO VESCOVO

This simple Renaissance church, all in brick, was previously a Veneto-Byzantine building that itself had replaced an even earlier structure, possibly founded in the 8th century. Sansovino was asked to rebuild San Martino to suit the growing population near the Arsenale. Although he used many of the earlier foundations, his reworking was fairly sweeping. He re-oriented the church so that the entrance faced the *campo*, and used the Greek-cross design instead of a long nave (the de' Barbari map of 1500 reveals its original shape; see Glossary, page 0.29). Research has shown that the original building contract stipulated whitewash for both interior and exterior walls. The present ceiling and wall decoration are 18th century. The outstanding interior feature is the 15th-century altar by Lorenzo Bregno, with carved angels by Tullio Lombardo (1511), originally housed in the oratory in the Tuscan town of Sansepolcro.

Today's façade is plain but was originally much plainer – the discreet Istrian stone detailing was added in the 19th century. Sansovino died before the church was completed and it remained unfinished until 1663. Despite this history of piecemeal construction, the church has a pleasing unity.

The adjoining oratory on the corner, now the parish office, has three oval windows facing the canal. The campanile, with blind Veneto-Byzantine arches on its upper levels, is 14th century. Look up the Fondamenta del Piovan o Erizzo for an oblique view of the land gate of the Arsenale – the brick of San Martino matches it beautifully.

LOCATION Campo San Martino, near the Arsenale
VAPORETTO Arsenale
ACCESS open daily, 9.00–11.45, 17.00–18.00; Sunday and holidays, 9.00–11.45

Jacopo Sansovino 1553

SAN PIETRO IN CASTELLO

Before working in Venice, Palladio was renowned as the architect of country villas for the Vicenzan nobility. In Venice, he became highly influential in church design. This church, Palladio's first Venetian project, evolved into the city's patriarchal cathedral and remained the seat of the Church until 1807. In 1556 the patriarch Vincenzo Diedo commissioned Palladio to rebuild the medieval structure. He drew up the plans, but Diedo's untimely death meant the project was postponed until Francesco Smeraldi executed them much later, in fact modifying them considerably. Nevertheless, like the façade of the Redentore, one temple breaks out of another which breaks out of another, a scheme reflecting the three naves inside and an important Palladian innovation.

The interior, a Latin cross, is a lumpen disappointment. The heavily decorated Vendramin chapel was designed by Longhena, as was the high altar (1649), built by Clemente Moli. More exciting is the marble model of the throne of St Peter (842–67), given to the doge of Venice in the late 13th century by Michele Paleologo, the then Eastern emperor.

The campanile is by Codussi. Built in 1482–90, it is faced entirely in Istrian stone – an innovation for its time. A contemporary called it '…powerful, isolated, crystal-white. Immobile at its base, yet in movement up there amongst the clouds… It is a sculpture caught between entrapment and flight… '. It now leans precariously towards the medieval cloisters (found through the opening marked No. 70), its present cupola dating from 1670.

LOCATION Campo San Pietro, reached from Via Garibaldi, past some lovely examples of vernacular architecture of all periods
VAPORETTO Giardini
ACCESS open Monday to Saturday, 10.00–17.30; Sunday, 15.00–17.30

Andrea Palladio/Francesco Smeraldi/Mauro Codussi (campanile) 1557–1621

CASA DELLA MARINAREZZA

Fronting the Riva dei Sette Martiri, and built to house sailors who had distinguished them-selves in naval service, the Casa della Marinarezza is a striking example of the Venetian Republic's almshouses. There is a certain irony that those occupants, who must have looked back on a lifetime in the golden age of Venice's maritime empire, would today be overlooking, and indeed often be dwarfed by, the massive cruise liners that regularly moor directly opposite.

The original 15th-century accommodation provided 55 dwellings in the three parallel three-storey blocks running back from the waterfront. Structure is exposed brickwork with stone detailing to windows and doors, eaves and quoining. On the side façade – go down the Corte de le Colonne – a rhythm of chimneys breaks through the façade. Although much altered over the centuries, you can still see that between the chimneys which divide the building into terraced apartments the windows were once symmetrically placed. At first-floor level all windows were arched – with two single and one pair per bay. The delicacy of those that remain can be seen in counterpoint to the massive brickwork of the chimney stacks. The more simply detailed front block was added 200 years later. This lacks a *piano nobile* and the openness of the original structure, presenting a utilitarian waterfront façade pierced by two arched entrances to the Corte de le Colonne behind.

CASTELLO

LOCATION Riva dei Sette Martiri
VAPORETTO Giardini
ACCESS not open to the public

15th/17th centuries

OSPEDALETTO
SANTA MARIA DEI DERELITTI

If you hate baroque architecture, then Longhena's façade (1670), a late work considered tasteless even at the time, will confirm you in your prejudices. Ruskin deemed it, along with San Moisè, Santa Maria del Giglio and other exuberances, 'illustrative of the last degradation of the Renaissance'. It is, nevertheless, theatrical and amusing, reminiscent of the powerful Pesaro monument in the Frari, and quite a statement on this restricted site. The façade was funded by a merchant, Bartolomeo Cargnoni, who stipulated in his will that it should be 'notable'. And so it is – with grotesque masks hanging over the pilasters on the lower order, and caryatids by Juste Le Court holding up the cornice above the second order.

Behind the church is the old hospice, established after the plague in 1527 as a charitable foundation, along with the Pietà, Incurabili and Mendicanti. The Ospedaletto housed poor and sick women. In 1662, Giuseppe Sardi restructured parts of this building. Not much of his work is left now, because Longhena was brought in after a row caused Sardi to pack his bags. Longhena completed the beautiful oval staircase and then overhauled the church, extending the choir and adding marble altars – including the lavish high altar – so giving the interior some continuity with the façade.

The charitable foundations were famous for providng women with a musical education. In 1777, a pretty, frescoed (recently restored) new music room designed by Matteo Lucchesi, was added to the hospice.

LOCATION on the Barbaria delle Tole near Campo dei Santi Giovanni e Paolo
VAPORETTO Ospedale
ACCESS open Thursday to Saturday, October to March, 15.00–18.0; April to September, 16.00–19.00. For the music room, ask the sacristan or try to attend a concert (often free)

Giuseppe Sardi 1662–66 / Baldassare Longhena 1666–72 / Matteo Lucchesi 1777

VIA GARIBALDI

The traditional Venetian island urban landscape comprises *campi* (squares – see Campo Bandiera e Moro, page 3.10) interconnected by *calli* (paths) or *salizzade* (streets). All are uniquely Venetian terms. With the exception of the 20th-century development of the Lido, the *via* (street) is an alien term from the mainland, redolent of outsiders. Via Garibaldi, originally named Eugenia, is unique – a straight thoroughfare, almost 20 metres wide, which cuts through the area of Castello adjacent to the Arsenale. It was created, on the instructions of Napoleon, by infilling a canal, its width thus taking in the canal and adjacent *fondamente*. Immediately afterwards, in 1810, its designer – Selva – laid out the connecting *viale* (avenue) and public gardens, created through wholesale demolition and appropriation of former monastic land. (See also Biennale Pavilions, page 3.42.) What we have today, therefore, is the typical amalgam of Venetian architecture, set into a new and unfamiliar context. At No. 1581 Via Garibaldi is an elegant example of a minor 15th-century palace (the third floor is a 17th-century addition); at No. 1310 is a beautiful, recently restored 14th-century hospital gateway. However, the areas adjacent to Via Garibaldi are largely unchanged despite Napoleon's grandiose urban plans. Look, for example, at Nos. 1980–1982 and 2018–2026 in the Calle dei Preti to the north, or the route out to San Pietro in Castello via Calle Crociera at the eastern end of Via Garibaldi, adjacent to the Rio Sant' Anna. The latter leads through typical areas of 15th–17th-century terraced housing of the *arsenalotti* (dockyard workers).

LOCATION Via Garibaldi
VAPORETTO Arsenale/Giardini
ACCESS public access

Giannantonio Selva early 19th-century street plan

CORPO DI GUARDIA

The neoclassical architectural style seen in the last years of the Republic was to become the style of Venice's French occupying forces after its fall in 1797 (see the Ala Napoloenica and the Coffee House). Neoclassicism was to continue under Venice's subsequent Austrian occupation of 1815–66.

This example, the Corpo di Guardia, is severely and symmetrically neoclassical, using the unadorned Doric order for the columns framing the entrance and supporting a heavy cornice. There is an austere beauty in the precision of its detailing, stripped as it is of any decorative ornamentation. Windows are punched out of the flat plane of its tightly jointed stonework, eased only by the most understated of mouldings. A stark statement to emphasise the grip of the Austrian military, it nestles by the brick walls of the Arsenale, where the occupying forces, in the interests of strengthening the defences of the city, had made various alterations, all under the direction of the architect Giovanni Casoni.

Intended to demonstrate and reinforce the authority of the Austrians, today it is an unthreatening single-storey construction, behind which the traditional Venetian brick crenellations topping the old Arsenale walls tower over it in symbolic superiority.

LOCATION on the corner of the Fondamenta dell'Arsenale and the Campo della Tana, under the walls of the Arsenale
VAPORETTO Arsenale
ACCESS not open to the public

Giovanni Casoni 1832

BIENNALE PAVILIONS

The public gardens which today house this series of exhibition pavilions were created by Napoleon as part of city-wide plans for transforming Venice's urban landscape and, arguably, to encourage loyalty to the occupying forces among the Arsenale workforce who predominantly lived in this area. Following its liberation in 1866 and absorption into the newly formed Italian nation, Venice needed to re-establish a unique presence. The creation of the Biennale in 1895 was meant to reinforce Venice's burgeoning reputation as a fashionable tourist destination. Originally intended as a showcase for Italian art, it soon became international, with exhibiting nations creating their individual pavilions. The result today is an 'expo-style' site of more than 20 pavilions, including a number by eminent architects – the pavilions of Finland (Alvar Aalto, 1956), Venezuela (Carlo Scarpa, 1954), Austria (Joseph Hoffman, 1934), Holland (Gerrit Rietveld, 1954), Japan (Y Takamasa, 1956) and Australia (Philip Cox, 1988) represent a snapshot of developing 20th-century architectural styles. However, a specific building's relevance can quickly fade as the needs and aspirations of exhibitors change over subsequent years. Some pavilions – notably the Italian – have been reworked many times to reflect this. The most recent addition is not a national pavilion but the 1991 Biennale bookshop by British architect James Stirling. Likened by many to an oversized *vaporetto*, its sweeping green copper roof and white-rendered entrance enclose a warm internal structure of delicately detailed wood and steel. An architecture biennale has recently been inaugurated, encouraging the pavilions' annual use.

LOCATION Giardini di Castello
VAPORETTO Giardini
ACCESS gardens open all year, pavilions only open during the Biennale

CASTELLO

various architects 1895–1991

MONUMENTO ALLA PARTIGIANA

Sprawled on the ground at the water's edge, her hands up by her face, one over the other, her dishevelled hair and figure undulating like the Venetian waves that lap over and around her, this figure of a partisan woman is both an object of universal pity and a symbol of Venetian strength. *La partigiana* is connected to the bank of the public gardens by a flight of steps made of separate Istrian stone cubes and designed by Carlo Scarpa and Sergio Los in 1968. The sculpture, cast in bronze by August Murer, replaces a previous terracotta piece by Leoncilli, which was destroyed by Fascists.

The initial idea had been to place the sculpture on a floating base, so that the figure would rise and fall with the waters of the Lagoon and be a constant reminder of all those Italian partisan women who risked their lives for their country. The version finally realised, however, appears and disappears with the changing level of the Lagoon and is no less effective for that.

Other modern sculptures are worth seeking out. One of the most powerful is Marino Marini's *Angel of the City* (1948), the equestrian figure located in front of the Guggenheim Collection (Palazzo Venier dei Leoni on the Grand Canal opposite the Palazzo Corner della Ca' Grande).

LOCATION Riva dei Partigiani, in front of the Giardini Pubblici
VAPORETTO Giardini
ACCESS public access

August Murer (sculptor), Carlo Scarpa and Sergio Los (architects) 1970

PALAZZO QUERINI STAMPALIA

Ever since it was built around 1520, the Querini Stampalia has been subject to revision and extension and is perhaps the ultimate expression of the Venetian penchant for such reworking. Behind an understated 16th-century façade with 18th-century interiors can now be found the work of Carlo Scarpa, Valeriano Pastor and Mario Botta.

The first indication of contemporary intervention is Scarpa's minimal wood and steel bridge access from the Campiello Querini Stampalia. Although no longer the public point of entry, this leads into the main ground-floor room, clad in travertine and incorporating both contemporary and classical Istrian stone detailing. Scarpa has channelled water through this space to the rear garden courtyard – reworked in a Moorish tradition. Pastor's work is found throughout the upper levels, providing a structural framework for the buildings through the insertion of a series of laminated timber beams. Most striking is his full-height stairwell – a highly elegant steel structure supporting green terrazzo stair treads and landings. The whole is then enclosed in timber cladding with porthole windows borrowing from the lightwell. Where Scarpa's work makes reference to Venetian design through a subtle layering of traditional elements, Pastor's presents bold contrast.

The most recent intervention, by Mario Botta, is the ground-floor central atrium, bookshop and cafeteria. He is also responsible for a new, second staircase, which wraps around a lift tower of polished black plaster with pink marble and stainless-steel detailing.

The building houses a museum of 18th-century interiors, a library and art bookshop.

LOCATION Rio di Santa Maria Formosa, off Campo Santa Maria Formosa
VAPORETTO Rialto/San Zaccaria
ACCESS open Tuesday to Sunday, 10.00–13.00, 15.00–18.00

Carlo Scarpa, Valeriano Pastor, Mario Botta (20th-century remodelling)

CITY HOSPITAL

In few places can the historic complexity, richness and interaction of Venice's physical and social structure be seen as clearly as it is here. Shortly after the Republic's fall in 1797, Napoleon designated the site of the Scuola Grande di San Marco to be the City Hospital. It was part of his programme to control the power of both the Church and the confraternities – the *scuole* (see Introduction, pages 0.11–0.14) – through systematic dissolution and closure. Also annexed were the former Dominican convent building associated with the adjoining Santi Giovanni e Paolo and Scamozzi's church of San Lazzaro dei Mendicanti.

Today the complex is still entered through the former *scuola* which, through a series of Renaissance corridors, leads the vistor to the new buildings at the rear. In 1978 phased redevelopment started with the new in-patient department. Laid out in the form of a cloister with an open arcaded ground floor, its barrel-shaped roofing reflects the Codussian precedent seen in the *scuola*'s façade. Further allusions to Venetian tradition may be found in the oculi – here seen as round and square alternating windows – and the use of polychromatic marble cladding and inserts. To the rear, the wing's external stair tower echoes the shape of the apse of the great church beyond. Later phases have added a variety of new accommodation including, most recently, the accident and emergency water gate to the Fondamente Nuove defined by a massive stone-clad arch and connected to the water-ambulance dock by an enclosed ramp with an undulating canopy – a reference to the Lagoon beyond.

LOCATION Campo dei Santi Giovanni e Paolo/Fondamente Nuove
VAPORETTO Ospedale
ACCESS visitors can walk through freely

Luciano Semerani and Gigetta Tamaro 1978–

DORSODURO

SAN NICOLÒ DEI MENDICOLI

Allegedly, San Nicolò was founded in the 7th century by Paduans fleeing the Longobards. It was reconstructed in the 12th century. Although much altered – particularly in the 1580s when some unfortunate gilding and gloomy paintings were added – it retains its basilical nave and columns (with 14th-century capitals) and has an atmospheric interior. It was last restored by the Venice in Peril Fund in the 1970s. The 15th-century portico was once a meeting place for *pizochere,* penitent ex-prostitutes. (San Giacometto is the only other Venetian church with a surviving portico.) The area housed a community of poor fishermen and sailors (*mendicoli* means 'beggars') and the people from here are still called *Nicolotti*.

The Istrian stone portal on the side façade was added in the 1850s and is now the church's main entrance. Inside, inspired lighting silhouettes the statues of angels on the altar and these, along with the 15th-century iconostasis supported by two sets of triple columns and topped with statues, do much for the atmosphere. Also notable are the wooden sculptures of the column capitals and the swirling timber brackets to the organ.

In the *campo,* a column bearing the lion of St Mark indicates the status of the *Nicolotti,* oarsmen to the doge. The campanile, struck by a stray shell during the Second World War, is 13th century. The adjoining oratory of San Filippo Neri, with an 18th-century doorway, was being restored in 2001. Scenes from Nicolas Roeg's *Don't Look Now* (1973), were filmed here. (See also the restored 19th-century cotton mill fronting the adjacent Fondamenta Bari, which houses departments of Venice's School of Architecture.)

LOCATION Fondamenta Tron
VAPORETTO San Basilio
ACCESS open daily, 10.00–12.00, 16.00–18.00

12th–16th centuries, last restored 1970s

PALAZZO ARIAN

44

Unmarked on most maps, the Palazzo Arian is immediately remarkable for its unique, six-lighted second-floor panel facing on to the *fondamenta*. This comprises a complex double layer of stonework quatrefoil tracery over trefoil, Gothic-arched windows. It creates a fully fretted appearance which, although somewhat naive in design conception, is among the earliest examples of the Venice's secular Gothic style which was to come to dominate its 15th-century architecture. The building layout is typical of the period – an L-shaped plan around the entrance courtyard with an external staircase leading to the upper floor. The upper storey oversails on timber beam supports forming a ground-floor portico.

The building was rebuilt in this form in the 14th century and is thought by some commentators to predate the façade of the Palazzo Ducale. The Arian family, whose coats of arms can be seen within the panels of the main window, was one of the oldest and most prosperous merchant families in Venice and had, since the 9th century, owned much of the surrounding area. Its standing in society was so great that when, in 1297, the list of those families who formed Venice's ruling Grand Council was closed, and restricted to noble families, the Arian, despite its bourgeois origins, was invited to join. However, by the time this building was constructed, the family had been expelled from the Grand Council owing to trading irregularities. It is quite likely, therefore, that the conception of this grand façade was intended as a direct snub to the ruling body.

LOCATION 2376 Fondamenta Briati opposite Rio di San Sebastiano
VAPORETTO San Basilio or Ca' Rezzonico
ACCESS not open to the public. Currently under restoration

mid 14th century

CA' DARIO

The picturesque Ca' Dario is part Venetian Gothic, part Renaissance. It is sometimes attributed to Pietro Lombardo, although no reliable records exist. It was originally a Gothic house, rebuilt in 1487 by Giovanni Dario, a diplomat rewarded by the Serenissima for facilitating the 1479 peace treaty with the Ottoman emperor. An inscription on the base translates as: 'To the Genius of the City [from] Joannes Darius'. The wording sidesteps *mediocritas*, the Venetian policy of discouraging individual self-aggrandisement.

Unusually, the Ca' Dario is detached. The ground-floor façade centres around a central arched doorway – but the upper storeys are asymmetrical, the windows interrupted by marble slabs decorated with roundels. The building sports Carpaccio-esque chimneys (so called because Carpaccio recorded their design in his paintings). Although not original here, the design of an inverted cone was uniquely Venetian, incorporating a cinder trap intended to minimise the risk of fire.

The Ca' Dario's recent social history is entwined with its architectural development. Lubbock Rawdon Brown, restorer of the Ca' Dario, killed himself here in 1883. In 1904 literary light Contessa de la Baume rebuilt the façade and added an iron balcony. In the mid 20th century it acquired a Moorish ballroom. 1979 saw Count Filippo Giordano delle Lanze killed here by his lover, and in 1993 the owner, Raul Gardini, shot himself in Milan. Not a lucky place!

LOCATION Grand Canal, not far from Santa Maria della Salute
VAPORETTO Salute
ACCESS not open to the public
VIEWPOINT from Campo del Traghetto, opposite bank of Grand Canal, near Campo Santa Maria del Giglio (*sestiere* San Marco)

possibly Pietro Lombardo 1487

PALAZZO CONTARINI DAL ZAFFO (POLIGNAC)

Seen from the Accademia bridge, this palace presents, in John Ruskin's words, 'a perfect and very rich example of Byzantine Renaissance' Venetian palazzo architecture. It belongs to the same transitional period between Gothic and Renaissance as Codussi's Palazzo Lando-Corner-Spinelli, with which it can be usefully compared. Here, however, the rigorous discipline of the symmetrical façade is lightened by its warm marble cladding and first-floor roundel insert panels which resonate with the nearby Ca' Dario. As is the case with that little palazzetto, no one knows which architect was responsible for the façade. The overall compostion and classical elements such as the fluted pilasters and garlanded first-floor frieze could be considered Codussian, whereas the decorative inlays are wholly Lombardesque. The latter attribution is supported by the diaries of 19th-century watercolourist John Bunney, who recorded that it was Pietro Lombardo, commissioned in 1480 by an eminent lawyer, who executed the design. Other commentators have ascribed the work to Giovanni Buora.

Rising from an Istrian-stone lower storey, the upper-level central multi-light windows are flanked by simple stone-framed windows within marble grounds. The resulting elegant and well-proportioned design relies for its effectiveness on an understated calm of contrasting geometric elements working on a flat façade. Over the following years, palace façades took on an increasing classical monumentality and sculptural depth – see for example Codussi's Palazzo Loredan-Vendramin-Calergi.

LOCATION Grand Canal
VAPORETTO Accademia
ACCESS not open to the public
VIEWPOINT Accademia bridge

?Pietro Lombardo/Mauro Codussi/Giovanni Buora late 15th century

SAN SEBASTIANO

The façade of Veronese's parish church now faces east on to the Rio San Sebastiano, next to the entrance to the university department of literature and philosophy (designed by Carlo Scarpa). Before Scarpagnino's 16th-century reconstruction, however (it was his last work), it faced the Campazzo San Sebastiano, which still provides a good view of the Veneto-Byzantine brick campanile and the sensual curves of the church. The all-stone façade, with its superimposed orders of columns and central round window, is reminiscent of Sante Lombardo's San Giorgio dei Greci.

The interior was decorated in 1555–70 by Veronese, who is buried here. His sumptuously clothed figures provide an earthly gloss on divine subjects and are at one both with his painted decoration of the church structure and with Scarpagnino's architecture. His *trompe l'oeil* work is impressive – particularly the twisted columns at clerestory level. Veronese trained as a stonecutter and also designed the high altar here. Architecturally, the big innovation was the choir gallery, which Scarpagnino extended to reach two-thirds of the way down the church. Such a layout was useful for accommodating choirs of different voices and was taken up by several other establishments. The fretwork on the gallery balustrade gives a pretty, airy feel to a structure that might otherwise have been overbearing in this space. The impressive statues on the gallery are by Girolamo Campagna.

For another view, walk through the university entrance into the courtyard.

LOCATION Campazzo San Sebastiano from Calle Avogaria or Fondamenta San Sebastiano, across the Rio di San Sebastiano
VAPORETTO San Basilio
ACCESS open daily, 10.00–15.00

Antonio Abbondi Scarpagnino/Girolamo Campagna (sculpture) 1508–48

CLOISTERS OF SANTA MARIA DELLA CARITÀ

This was the first of Palladio's designs actually to be built in Venice and, although unfinished, remains an extraordinarily powerful work. Originally constructed for the convent of the adjacent church of the Carità, since 1807 the buildings have housed Venice's art school and are now part of the Gallerie dell' Accademia.

Contemporary with the 'Romanisation' of Venetian secular architecture, Palladio created here a rigorously correct solution of superimposed Doric, Ionic and Corinthian orders – the seven-arched, lower-level open portico and loggia contrasting with the third level of smaller window openings. Although probably rooted in a limited budget, the use of brick for all but the specific details of column bases and capitals, first-floor balustrading and keystones and upper-level window surrounds, accentuates the power of the whole.

Palladio's overall intention had been to recreate a grand Roman house, based on the writings of Vitruvius, in which today's surviving wing would have been one side of an atrium (all as recorded in Palladio's *Four Books of Architecture*, 1570). However, its design also incorporates motifs within the terracotta frieze taken from Rome's Theatre of Marcellus and the Colosseum. Within the cloister is Palladio's recently restored former chapter house and elegant ovoid spiral staircase. His later work – seen at Redentore and San Giorgio Maggiore – was to depart from such a rigorous interpretation of ancient architectural principles.

LOCATION Campo della Carità

VAPORETTO Accademia

ACCESS currently no official public access, but visible from the Gallerie dell' Accademia (between rooms 20 and 21), which is open (summer hours) Monday, 9.00–14.00; Tuesday to Saturday, 9.00–22.00; Sunday, 9.00-19.00; (winter hours) daily, 9.00–19.00

Andrea Palladio 1552

PALAZZO BALBI

Palazzo Balbi heralds the baroque style that was to dominate 17th-century Venetian architecture. The 'Romanisation' of Venice, first seen in Sansovino's Palazzo Corner della Ca' Grande, was being consolidated, and echoes of that building can be seen in the oval attic-storey windows of the Palazzo Balbi. The strictly classical features of the Renaissance style are beginning to be modified by mannerist detail that will increasingly move towards the theatrical, exaggerated three-dimensional façades seen at, for instance, Ca' Pesaro and the Ospedaletto. Balbi's position at the bend of the Grand Canal ensures maximum visibility – further emphasised by the typically proto-baroque roof-top obelisks. The style is still restrained but baroque features are clearly evident – broken pediments now rise over the outer windows at upper levels and, at water level, tie the outermost windows to the two additional water gates (A palace intended for one owner would normally have only one, central water gate.) Florid coats of arms proclaim the self-importance of the palace's owner – Nicolò Balbi, governor of Mestre.

The family was to remain prominent in Venetian society – in literature and the arts – and, it is recorded, hosted Napoleon to watch the regatta held in his honour in 1807. (It is also interesting to note that, but for the opposition which led to its ultimate rejection, the adjoining site would now house Frank Lloyd Wright's 1953 proposed project for the Masieri Foundation, to accommodate students of the Venice School of Architecture.)

LOCATION Grand Canal/Corte del Remer
VAPORETTO San Tomà
ACCESS not open to the public (currently headquarters of the Veneto Regional Council)
VIEWPOINT Calle Giustinian (Dorsoduro)

Alessandro Vittoria 1582–90

SANTA MARIA DELLA SALUTE

Seen from a passing *vaporetto,* the statues of the Salute dance around the static figure of the Virgin perched at the pinnacle of its monumental dome, buttressed by huge spiral volutes. The architect, the 32-year-old Longhena, saw the form of the dome as a crown for Santa Maria della Salute (the Madonna of Health).

This is indeed a votive church, celebrating delivery from what was to prove the last great plague which, in 1630–31, claimed the lives of around 46,000 people – 30 per cent of Venice's population. A public work commissioned by the Senate, it was also to proclaim Venice's eternal fortune and autonomy from papal control. While its design draws on Palladian precedent seen at the Redentore, its tone rejects the latter's sombre, reverential feel and adopts an exuberant magnificence. Considered the defining building of 17th-century Venice, with it Longhena also created the setting for a unique piece of theatre. Each year the doge crossed from San Marco on a temporary pontoon bridge, sweeping through the central triumphal arch to give thanks for deliverance from the plague. (The event is still celebrated each November, albeit with no doge!)

Inside, the church's unique octagonal, centralised plan is easily read – six side chapels are expressed on the façade flanking the central triumphal-arched entrance, which in turn faces the altar, pulled out into a separately domed apse.

Construction of the church was a considerable logistical and technical challenge; it is allegedly supported by almost 1.2 million timber piles driven into the Lagoon floor.

LOCATION Grand Canal/Campo della Salute
VAPORETTO Salute
ACCESS open daily, 9.00–12.00, 15.00–17.00
VIEWPOINT not really necessary, but try Calle del Traghetto off Vialle 22 Marzo, San Marco

Baldassare Longhena 1631–81

SCUOLA GRANDE DEI CARMINI
SANTA MARIA DEL CARMELO

Founded in the 1590s in support of the Carmelite monastery nearby, the present building was started in 1625 by Francesco Caustello. Longhena added his delicately ornamented symmetrical façade, typical of early baroque taste, in 1668. In 1767, by this time popular and wealthy, as Carmelite foundations were throughout Europe, the *scuola* was upgraded to a *scuola grande* (see Introduction, pages 0.11–0.14).

Inside, the ceilings steal the show. Longhena's restrained barrel-vaulted double staircase is either gloriously enhanced or utterly spoilt (depending on your point of view) by Abbondio Stazio's rich stucco work added to the ceiling in 1728–29. (Stazio was responsible for similar work in the little sacristy on the lower floor.) Sirens, angels and floral decoration are all gilded in a flurry of 18th-century overkill. The archive hall has a heavily carved 16th-century timber ceiling, heaving with coloured inlaid wood and painted compartments. Also notable here are the 18th-century benches with inlaid walnut and the polychrome marble floor. A more delicate decorated ceiling, by Francesco Lucchini (1740), can be seen in the *albergo* – the small first-floor meeting room. The ceiling in the upstairs hall, as James Morris points out, 'glows and sometimes shrieks, with the talent of Tiepolo' – a cycle of nine paintings (1739–49). Tiepolo was made an honorary member of the *scuola* for this feat. The effect is currently slightly spoilt (2001) as the huge central painting has, according to a member of the ticket office staff, 'fallen down because of woodworm'.

LOCATION just off the Campo Santa Margherita, off Fondamenta del Soccorso
VAPORETTO San Basilio/Ca' Rezzonico
ACCESS open April to October, 9.00–18.00; Sundays; 9.00–13.00; November to March, 9.00–16.00; Sundays, 9.00–13.00

Francesco Caustello, Baldassare Longhena, Abbondio Stazio (stucco work) 1668–70

BOATYARD AT SAN TROVASO

This boatyard (*squero*), established in the 17th-century and the busiest of only four left in Venice, nestles by the church of San Trovaso. Before boat-building activities were mostly removed to the Arsenale in the early 14th century, it was these small boatyards that built and maintained the Venetian fleet.

In a city constructed almost entirely of brick and Istrian stone, this building is an anomaly. Looking more like three wooden lean-tos than a serious enterprise, but no less picturesque for that, it consists of a small workshop on the *rio* and more substantial living accommodation behind – light wooden structures supported on brick piers. The alpine feel of the building is no accident: boatyard workers came originally from the Dolomites and built their accommodation according to their own tradition.

Gondolas in for repair lie like a family of basking sharks in neat rows on the edge of the *rio*. The gondola is not a modern tourist trap but an ancient form of transport first appearing in the city's records in 1094 and taking its present form by the 18th century. Since the sumptuary laws of 1562, forbidding too much ostentatious display, all gondolas have been black. Lorenzo della Toffola, who runs the San Trovaso boatyard, makes only three or four gondolas a year, repairing and updating around 400 others. A gondola is composed of more than 200 different elements, and uses eight types of wood. The cost – more than €41,000 – goes some way to explain the extortionate hourly rates demanded of visitors.

LOCATION Fondamenta Nani, off the Fondamenta Ponte Lungo on the Zattere
VAPORETTO Zattere
ACCESS not officially open, but ask to look around. Clearly visible from across the *rio*

17th century

PALAZZO ZENOBIO

The long, understated stone façade of the Palazzo Zenobio does little to prepare the visitor for what lies behind – one of the most extraordinary baroque interiors in Venice. The wealthy Veronese Zenobio family had been granted their place in Venice's aristocracy in the mid 17th century owing to their considerable donation to Venice's fund for the war against Crete. Further consolidating their status through the marriage of a daughter into an 'old' Venetian family, they went on to buy this formerly Gothic palazzo and hired a young pupil of Longhena, Antonio Gaspari, to remodel it. The French frescoist Louis Dorigny and the Ticinese stuccoist Abbondio Stazio joined Gaspari, and this team was to create a perfect fusion of architecture, painting and sculpture in the Venetian late-baroque style, seen at its most exuberant in the first-floor ballroom.

Gaspari has reworked the traditional full-depth *pòrtego* to form a small hall open to the rear of the building only. To the front is the double-height ballroom with musicians' gallery. Look up and you are drawn into the receding planes of a corbelled *trompe l'oeil* framing Dorigny's fresco of Apollo and Aurora. Working down the walls, the *trompe l'oeil* seamlessly passes into extravagant panelled stucco work and vast mirrors. Allegorical references to the sun heralding a new dawn symbolically reflect the fortunes of the Zenobio family. However, shortly after the Republic's fall the Zenobio quit Venice; since 1850 the palace has been owned by the Armenian community.

In the grounds is Tommaso Temanza's (restored) late-18th-century library pavilion.

LOCATION 2596 Fondamenta del Soccorso
VAPORETTO Ca' Rezzonico/San Basilio
ACCESS interior can be viewed by appointment only: telephone 5228770, fax 5203434

Antonio Gaspari late 17th century

CASA TORRES

This perfect small Veneto-Byzantine palace lookalike, set in a little garden and built on two levels, is rather isolated and perhaps not completely at one with its more workaday surroundings on this quiet backwater. Nevertheless, it was obviously a labour of love and historical accuracy for its Venetian-born-and-bred architect-owner, who was also responsible for the very different, minimalist Santa Maria della Vittoria, built on the Lido some 15 years later. The historian Concina calls the Casa Torres 'a treasury of scrupulously accurate quotations', and notes that it is a virtual copy of a medieval house with workshop on the Campo Santa Margherita. With its pseudo-shop on the ground floor, an icon-type stained-glass window, an exaggerated gargoyle for taking water off the roof, an eclectic collection of chimneys, colourful brickwork, patterned tiles and balconies, the house is a delight to the eye, particularly when it is reflected in the waters of the *rio*.

From the Ponte Marcello, you can see the left-hand side of the house, with its small-scale cylindrical tower, topped with a lead dome over a cornice of patterned tiles. There is a loggia or covered balcony at the back of the house, overlooking the garden.

For an example of this style applied to mass housing, see Alessandri's Nardi Housing in *sestiere* San Marco.

DORSODURO

LOCATION Fondamenta del Gaffaro, a short stride from the Campo dei Frari
VAPORETTO San Tomà
ACCESS not open to the public

Giuseppe Torres 1905–08

PALAZZO STERN

The architectural fashion at the beginning of the 20th century was for painstakingly recreating the successful buildings of Venice's past, in particular Veneto-Byzantine buildings such as the Casa Torres and neo-Gothic palaces such as this one on the Grand Canal. The Palazzo Stern is a fake in that the distribution of the windows bears little or no relation to the living space behind them, and as such the building has come in for a certain amount of critical derision. As it is detached and singular, it has also been criticised for weakening the look of the canal.

Nevertheless, as a detailed historical exercise and an attractive decorative envelope, it succeeds. The Istrian stone windows and quoins, the balustrading on the upper level which is reflected in the terrace bordering the Grand Canal, the covered portico with its stone columns and the enclosed garden marked with Gothic detailing present a powerful reminder of an earlier age, one guaranteed to get a whole *vaporetto* load of tourists leaning eagerly over the side.

One of the best views is from the right-hand side, where there is an oriel window on the upper level, and a vast Gothic window that breaks through the façade at roof level. Here too, the precise detailing of the Istrian stone quoins is very apparent.

Berti collaborated with the painter and decorator Raffaele Mainella who worked on creating an interior with a suitably period feel.

LOCATION Grand Canal, next to Ca' Rezzonico
VAPORETTO Ca' Rezzonico
ACCESS not open to the public
VIEWPOINT San Samuele *traghetto* stop on the opposite bank

Giuseppe Berti 1909–12

BUILDINGS ON THE FONDAMENTA ZATTERE

In the first years of the 20th century there was a move to expand the city to outlying areas. Much of this new building was in the Gothic-revival style, thought by some commentators to have been fostered by the publication of Ruskin's *The Stones of Venice* in 1851–53. On the Lido building was less constrained by the city's illustrious past, but here on the broad and generous Fondamenta Zattere fronting the Giudecca Canal we see the final flush of nostalgia for pseudo-medieval Venetian palaces. Architecturally backward-looking they may be, but there is no denying the architects' historical knowledge.

The most distinctive examples are Sardi's painstakingly detailed house at No. 1386, built for the Scarpa family in 1911–12, and a palazzetto at No. 1413 by Giuseppe Berti (1912–14). Giovanni Sardi, a great neo-Gothicist, was also responsible for the Hotel Excelsior on the Lido. Next door, at No. 1411, modern windows have been inset in the Gothic-style surrounds, rather detracting from the mosaic panel advertising the Adriatica company. The gold lettering glittering on a blue mosaic background, a symbol of the riches of Venice nestling in its blue lagoon, is entirely appropriate for a company connected with shipping. (A new headquarters for Adriatica was built in 1957–59 on the Calle Larga XXII Marzo, *sestiere* San Marco, by Angelo Scattolin.)

Note the second-floor loggia at No. 1470, and the traditional *altana* at No. 1471. The stretch, which includes some neo-Renaissance buildings, continues down to No. 1485b.

LOCATION Fondamenta Zattere
VAPORETTO Zattere/San Basilio
ACCESS buildings not open to the public

Giovanni Sardi, Giuseppe Berti, and others early 20th century

CASA SALVIATI

In the 1920s and 1930s there was a certain amount of private building in the centre of Venice which resulted in this idiosyncratic house in a prominent position on the Grand Canal. In this period, the penchant for neo-Gothic buildings such as the Palazzo Stern, prevalent earlier in the 20th century, had given way to a more classical-revivalist style. Behind the eye-catching gaudy mosaics, Casa Salviati is an example of this.

A small palace, Casa Salviati was one of two houses built by dall'Olivo at this time. His other house is a much more modest construction built three years later on the Rio di San Vio, *sestiere* Dorsoduro. This second building is much preferred by architectual commentators while the Casa Salviati, built for Murano glassmakers of the same name, is derided for its ostentatious decoration, thought only too reminiscent of some of the less tasteful Venetian glass. On the other hand, such excess has its own Venetian tradition – the golden façade of the Ca' d'Oro must originally have been almost blinding, as must the now-lost murals by Giorgione and Titian on the façade of the Fondaco dei Tedeschi – and this small- scale palace can be seen as part of a Venetian tendency. The larger mosaic shows Victorians in romantic medieval dress cavorting under a Mucha-esque goddess. Below that are four smaller panels depicting nude painters.

DORSODURO

LOCATION on the Grand Canal, near the Ca' Dario
VAPORETTO Salute (but not for the façade, only the back entrance)
ACCESS not open to the public
VIEWPOINT Campo del Traghetto off the Campo Santa Maria del Giglio (San Marco)

G dall'Olivo 1924–26

FIRE STATION

Venice's fire station has, along with virtually every other 20th-century Venetian building, received its quota of derision and criticism from Italian architectural commentators. Its architectural style – seen by some as a precursor of the imminent Fascist interpretation of modernism – does, however, incorporate reference to a number of traditional Venetian design elements. Istrian stone frames the double order of windows, while the rusticated base with its four grand arched openings and exaggerated keystones recalls 16th-century baroque detailing. The latter arches of course hold the key to the building – moorings for the boats of Venice's fire brigade – and the fortunate visitor will witness the dramatic mobilisation of this water-borne force, its backwash bringing temporary chaos to the otherwise quiet *rio* at its junction with the Grand Canal.

The building's architect – then a lecturer at the Venice School of Architecture – was also responsible for the earlier Pharmacist's House on the Lido.

DORSODURO

LOCATION Rio di Ca' Foscari
VAPORETTO Ca' Rezzonico/San Tomà
ACCESS not open to the public

Brenno del Giudice 1932–34

PONTE DELL'ACCADEMIA

By the 1930s, the *vaporetti* ploughing up and down the Grand Canal had increased in size, and the need to replace the unloved, flat, industrial-looking iron bridge put up here by the Austrians in 1854 prompted the Venetians to hold a competition, presided over by Ugo Ojetti, for a suitable replacement.

Leading architects of the day put forward their designs, but none of these captured the imagination of the commission sufficiently to inspire them to give the go-ahead. In the end this wooden bridge by Miozzi (architect of the INA Garage) was put up as a temporary measure. Current architectural thinking is that this temporary bridge is better than any of the competition designs, that of Pica-Buccianti being judged 'grotesque', that of Pascoletti-Barducci-Borghi too modernistic, the Fagiuoli-Danusso too much like a motorway, and the Torres-Bisazza unresolved in its proportions.

Indeed the design of the current Ponte dell'Accademia is elegant, its technical structure admirable, its atmosphere suitably romantic and its position at the end of the tourist drag from the Piazza San Marco to the Gallerie dell'Accademia part of the modern myth of Venice. Stand on it by night and watch the moon on the water, and by day get a good view of the Palazzo Contarini dal Zaffo.

DORSODURO

LOCATION the route is marked clearly from Piazza San Marco, via Campo Francesco Morosini
VAPORETTO Accademia
ACCESS always open

Eugenio Miozzi 1932

APARTMENT BUILDING, ZATTERE

4.36

This building of 18 apartments exemplifies the difficulty of finding appropriate architectural language for a modern development near the centre of Venice that achieves historical continuity without resorting to revivalism. The Istrian stone detailing to the window surrounds and balconies, and pierced decorative glazing to the side façades and base show a sensitivity and allusion to Venetian tradition. A wellhead provides the focus for the internal central courtyard. However, viewed from a distance there seems little regard for urban context – its scale overwhelms the adjacent housing and the Renaissance church of Spirito Santo. In addition, quirks of its form – such as second- and third-floor windows which apparently arbitrarily move off alignment, and a sixth-floor balcony cantilevered on all sides – seem ill-considered and unsatisfying, neither conforming to the expectation of a load-bearing structure, nor exploiting the design potential of what is actually a framed building structure. Undifferentiated window proportions, baldly reflecting the unified internal function, do little to relieve the lack of visual coherence. In its function it may be compared with the revivalist Nardi housing, built 50 years earlier.

DORSODURO

LOCATION Zattere allo Spirito Santo/
Calle dello Zuccaro, Dorsoduro 4012
VAPORETTO Zattere
ACCESS only if you live here

Ignazio Gardella 1954–58

SAN MARCO

SAN MARCO

Not the seat of the Roman Catholic church in Venice, but the doge's private chapel and shrine to St Mark – this was the purpose of the basilica of San Marco throughout the years of the Venetian Republic. It was only with Napoleon's conquest that, in 1807 – as a clear signal of the dismantling of the institutions of the Republic – San Marco was declared successor to the physically remote Venetian cathedral of San Pietro in Castello.

From its inception in the 9th century, the basilica had proclaimed the doge's role not just as secular leader of Venice, but also as defender of the Christian faith – Venetian triumph in war adding to the glory of their Republic's religious benefactor, the evangelist St Mark. In this perception the doge considered himself a legitimate rival to the pope holding court in the Vatican – a belief that would cause repeated conflict between Venice and the Church of Rome. The body of St Mark had been smuggled out of Alexandria, arriving in Venice in 829, an event immortalised in Tintoretto's painting of the subject (now in the Accademia). Immediately, a modest chapel was erected adjacent to the church of the then patron of Venice – the Greek St Theodore.

The structure seen today was created in the 11th century. Its form – the five-domed Greek cross – takes its inspiration from the eastern Christian church, and may be compared to the 6th-century Apostoleion built by Emperor Justinian in Constantinople. Its early function as a mausoleum for successive doges echoes the burial tradition of Roman emperors in the Apostoleion. For a 13th-century view of the basilica, study the mosaic facing the Piazza San Marco over the far left doorway. The only original external mosaic, this shows the façade without its later upper-level Gothic additions, but includes the four bronze horses brought back after the fall of Constantinople in 1204 and now housed in a special room within the basilica. (The horses seen on the façade today are replicas.) Note also the exceptionally fine 13th-century sculpted arches to the central doorway. The soffit

11th–19th centuries

carvings to the outermost arch show a range of Venetian trades; it is said that the first figure on the left side depicts the basilica's architect – lame because such genius must be
paid for, and biting his nails for fear that his work may not live up to expectation.

Internally, the mood is distinctly oriental – where Torcello's Santa Maria Assunta is
reminiscent of the basilical churches of Rome and the Western Roman Empire, San Marco
evokes the architecture of Constantinople and the East. Until the 12th century, the interior
would have felt even more mysterious than it does today. The side aisles were floored
over at high level – a feature only recalled today by the residual walkways – to provide
segregated women's galleries and greatly reducing light to the main floor. Over subsequent centuries the building was increasingly embellished with gold and mosaics, inside
and out, ostensibly to honour its patron saint, but effectively demonstrating the growing
temporal power of the Venetian Republic, and legitimising an extraordinary collection of
the spoils of war.

LOCATION Piazza San Marco
VAPORETTO San Marco/San Zaccaria
ACCESS open daily, 6.30–17.30

11th–19th centuries

PALAZZO DUCALE

For almost a thousand years the Palazzo Ducale housed the complete mechanisms of Venetian government. Within its interiors are stupendous spaces meant to strike awe into visiting delegations and terror into any citizen who contravened the laws of the Republic. Even today, to tour the austere accommodation that housed the torture chambers and detention rooms interwoven with the ostentatious public rooms is to experience another, sinister side to the governing Serenissima.

The palazzo comprises three wings ranged round an internal court, respectively housing the legislature and its courts (facing the Piazzetta), the vast meeting room of the Grand Council (facing the waterfront), and the doge's private quarters, ancillary administrative offices and meeting rooms (facing the adjacent canal). This layout existed by the 12th century, when the palazzo would have resembled a Veneto-Byzantine *fondaco* similar to the Fondaco Dei Turchi. Its subsequent physical deterioration – hastened by the repeated fires that seemed to dog the complex – combined with the Republic's growing need for enlarged administrative accommodation, meant that by the 14th century the palazzo required rebuilding. Starting around 1340, the process – one wing at a time – was to continue for more than 200 years. Today's external public face epitomises the Venetian Gothic style and, in particular, incorporates the innovative structural device of the circular quatrefoil stone tracery interwoven over trefoil Gothic ogee arching. You can almost see the structural forces snaking their way through this complex arching. The Palazzo Ducale maintains the open façade much favoured in Venice, but transcends the relatively static rhythm of, for example, Ca' Loredan and Ca' Farsetti to create a dynamic and uniquely Venetian assimilation of the flowing geometry of Islamic design and the structural ambition of European Gothic. This motif would thereafter be replicated, in a variety of adapted forms, by palaces throughout the city (see Ca' d'Oro, Palazzo Pisani-Moretta,

B Bon, A Rizzo, P Lombardo, G Spavento, G Scarpagnino 14th–16th centuries

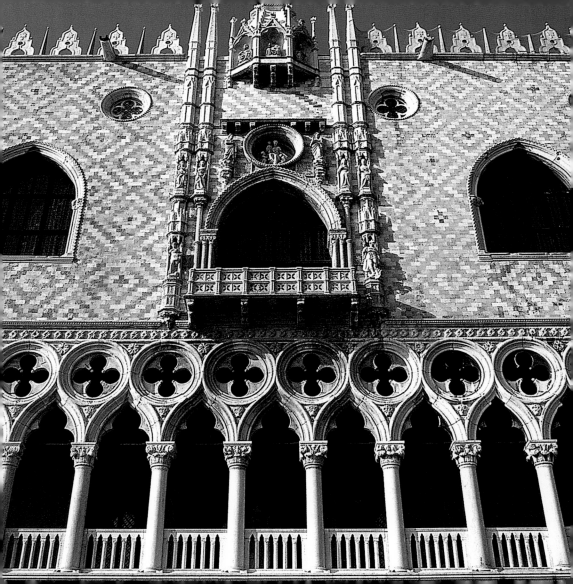

5.8

and Palazzo Mastelli). The building's massing also defies structural convention, and so creates further visual tension, by placing a solid upper storey over the two levels of continuous open arcades.

For Ruskin the palazzo represented the 'model of all perfection ... a magnificent arrangement of all that is in building most dignified'. Three centuries earlier Palladio had seen it differently, arguing, in his proposals for the building's demolition following extensive fire damage, that its massing 'offended all natural principles'. The inherent caution of the Republic prevailed and the façades were retained. Today the only external evidence of the disastrous fire is the absence of stone tracery within the second-floor windows.

Integral to these façades is an exceptional cycle of 14th-century sculpture. Thirty-six column capitals record scenes of vice and virtue. Numerically identified from the far right of the water frontage, capital 24 – crowning a slightly thicker column – marks the end of the first wing to be rebuilt; it records eight episodes in a couple's life from courtship to the birth of their child. Above this level – at the corners – are the Drunkenness of Noah, under the Archangel Raphael, and Adam and Eve, under the Archangel Michael; the latter, as archangel of punishment, a fitting image to face the columns of St Theodore and St Mark – site of public executions. At the third corner the Judgement of Solomon makes reference to the legislature that this wing housed.

Finally, in 1438–42, a formal, ceremonial entrance was added – the Porta Della Carta – designed by Bartolomeo Bon, and considered the ultimate expression of Venetian Gothic architecture. Above the exuberant traceried window is mounted a bust depicting St Mark the evangelist. Below, the figure of the contemporary doge, Francesco Foscari, kneels before Venice's symbolic depiction of the saint – the winged lion. (This is a 19th-century copy – the original is in the palace's musem.)

SAN MARCO

B Bon, A Rizzo, P Lombardo, G Spavento, G Scarpagnino 14th–16th centuries

PALAZZO DUCALE/DOGE'S PALACE

Here begins a grand processional route to the inner courtyard, through a colonnade externally styled in a strangely hybrid pinnacled confection of Gothic and Renaissance, and up a grand external staircase into the first floor of the last wing to be reconstructed – the east. Started by Antonio Rizzo in the 1480s, and completed by Lombardo, Spavento and Scarpagnino some 40 years later, this stone-clad wing epitomises the delicate, richly decorated Venetian-Renaissance style. Its lower levels maintain the arcaded loggias of the first two wings, reworked in transitional Gothic-Renaissance form, but rising above this is a lively rhythm of openings and bas-relief carving whose character is in marked contrast to the former two wings. Finally, in the 1560s, Sansovino's two giant figures of Neptune and Mars – symbolic of Venice's maritime strength – were added to the grand staircase.

LOCATION Piazzetta San Marco
VAPORETTO San Marco/San Zaccaria
ACCESS interiors open (summer), 9.00–19.00; (winter) 9.00–16.00

B Bon, A Rizzo, P Lombardo, G Spavento, G Scarpagnino 14th–16th centuries

MARCIANA LIBRARY

In 1545, while Sansovino was building the library, a section of the colonnade ceiling collapsed. He was thrown into jail. Later released, he had to pay for the damage and replace the vaulting with a coffered timber ceiling more suited to Venice's unstable foundations. Notwithstanding this setback, Sansovino's understanding of Roman architectural principles and mythology produced a masterpiece here. Facing the Palazzo Ducale and defining the Piazzetta San Marco, the library's strongly horizontal façade with two superimposed orders – Ionic over Doric – honoured the Republic as a seat of humanist learning. It housed the priceless book collection of Cardinal Bessarion (1396–1472) and Petrarch's library, left to the Republic in the 14th century and hitherto shamefully neglected.

Particularly innovative are the statue-rich parapet and the way the frieze wraps around the corner of the façade – showing Sansovino's skill in adapting Vitruvian principles. The building was completed by Scamozzi after Sansovino died in 1556.

The ground-floor entrance caryatids and the staircase are by Alessandro Vittoria (1553–55). The vestibule and main hall are both by Sansovino, but when Giovanni Grimani bequeathed his remarkable collection of antiquities to the State in 1587, Scamozzi refashioned the vestibule to house it. Most of this collection is now in the Archaeological Museum. The elaborate main hall still holds some incunabula. The floor comes from Sansovino's Scuola Grande della Misericordia – relaid here in 1815 for the visit of Francis I. The paintings decorating the coffered ceiling and walls are by leading Venetian artists.

LOCATION Piazzetta San Marco

VAPORETTO San Marco

ACCESS open daily, April to October, 9.00-19.00; November to March, 9.00-17.00. Entrance only with *biglietto cumulativo*, available at Museo Correr

Jacopo Sansovino and Vincenzo Scamozzi 1537–53

PIAZZA SAN MARCO, PIAZZETTA SAN MARCO AND IL MOLO

Since the early 9th century, the political and spiritual powerbase of the Venetian Republic has been located in the Piazza and Piazzetta San Marco. Chosen for its firm ground and adjacent deepwater harbour, its form, with the exception of its western enclosure – the Ala Napoleonica – remains unchanged since the 16th century. It is easy to be impressed by the buildings that are now primarily tourist attractions without appreciating the historical power of this unique piece of cityscape, and the basis of its design. It is a sequence of spaces intended to be approached from the Lagoon – traditionally from the Adriatic via the navigable channel through the natural barriers of the Lido – but for today's visitors, who mostly arrive at the Piazzale Roma or the railway station, this experience is often lost. They approach the Piazza San Marco via the Grand Canal.

The Palazzo Ducale – initially a moated castle – stood on the site of the current building, its flank facing a small harbour rather than today's paved Piazzetta. The land for the Piazzetta was reclaimed in the 12th century, the broad quay of Il Molo created and the resulting grand approach formalised with the two vast columns crowned by the Republic's patron saints – the Greek St Theodore, and St Mark, symbolised by the winged lion. Henceforth, this space was the political heart of the Republic. Its drama and power would be increasingly consolidated – first by the 14th-century reconstruction and enlargement of the Palazzo Ducale, and then in the 16th century by the Marciana Library opposite.

The divergent enclosure of the Piazzetta leads the eye on to the Piazza itself – its entrance framed by the campanile and south façade of San Marco. This façade was the one seen from the Lagoon, and so was the most richly decorated. It includes the imperial sculpture of the four tetrarchs and two imposing freestanding columns looted from Acre. The axis of this view now centres on the late-15th-century clocktower, attributed to Mauro Codussi, which marks the entrance to the main commercial street leading to the Rialto – a

B Bon, M Codussi, J Sansovino, V Scamozzi, B Longhena

PIAZZA SAN MARCO, PIAZZETTA SAN MARCO AND IL MOLO

view further defined by the three bronze flagpoles raised in 1505. This, therefore, is the architectural drama that the Republic created as its face to the world, not the relatively static view of the basilica from the Piazza that is most commonly admired today.

In contrast to the Piazzetta, the Piazza represented the spiritual role of the Republic. It accommodated the procurators, who were appointed directly by the doge and were responsible for the management of the basilica and its shrine. Their 12th-century accommodation along the north side of the Piazza – the Procuratie Vecchie – was rebuilt, following a fire in 1512, and a third storey added, albeit consistent in style with its Veneto-Byzantine predecessor. In 1529, the procurators appointed Jacopo Sansovino as their architect, in succession to Bon (from Bergamo). Sansovino's subsequent proposals radically reviewed and formalised both the Piazza and Piazzetta. The line of the south side of the Piazza was redrawn, widening towards the basilica and so leaving its campanile detached, its base embellished with a new loggetta. A motley grouping of market buildings and almshouses then facing the Procuratie Vecchie and Palazzo Ducale were demolished, leaving Sansovino free to create his Romanised vision for the heart of the Republic. By his death in 1570 only one element – the magnificent Marciana Library – had been largely built. It was to be Vincenzo Scamozzi, succeeded by Baldassare Longhena, who would complete Sansovino's plan for the Piazza enclosure with the Procuratie Nuove – a monumental structure, criticised from the outset for its addition of a third storey looming above the adjacent library.

LOCATION Piazza San Marco
VAPORETTO San Marco/San Zaccaria

B Bon, M Codussi, J Sansovino, V Scamozzi, B Longhena

ALA NAPOLEONICA

The western enclosure of the Piazza San Marco is a Napoleonic creation. It was part of an unrealised masterplan to eradicate all memory of the Republic and transform the Procuratie Nuove into a royal palace worthy of Venice's new role as the second capital of Napoleon's Italian empire. This frontage had been part of Sansovino's 16th-century remodelling of the Piazza – the wings of the Procuratie Vecchie and Nuove returning to buttress a classically redesigned façade to the church of San Germignano. These were totally demolished, to be replaced by today's unifying wing, and creating a new access point into the Piazza.

The design of the first and second storeys of the Piazza frontage replicates that of the adjacent Procuratie Nuove, somewhat less satisfactorily joining with the Procuratie Vecchie. Above these, however, is a deep blind storey with decorative frieze and statues portraying Roman emperors. At its centre can be seen the space, never filled, intended to house a similar statue of Napoleon. The function of this storey is to mask the roofline of the double-storey ballroom that the Ala Napoleonica houses. The building's rear façade is neoclassical, with rusticated lower-storey arcade and frieze, reminiscent of Santi's Coffee House, and a giant first-floor order of Ionic pilasters, facing the even more severe neoclassicism of Santi's guardhouse (today's post office). The interior, designed by Soli, contains a monumental staircase rising to the recently restored magnificent ballroom and ancillary rooms decorated in neoclassical style.

LOCATION Piazza San Marco
VAPORETTO San Marco
ACCESS public access to exhibitions (Correr Museum)

Giuseppe Soli and Lorenzo Santi 1810–15

CAFFÈ FLORIAN

Today, the clientèle of this historic Venetian establishment, with its distinctive shuttered façade complete with 19th-century lettering, is neither subversive nor particularly elegant, but the caffè has a colourful history. During the revolutionary years of 1848–49, Florians was a hotbed of radical action against the Austrian occupiers. Venetians wounded in a confrontation on 18 March, 1848 in the Piazza San Marco, were carried back to the Caffè Florian. In the 19th century, Balzac termed the place 'at once a stock exchange, a theatre foyer, a reading room, a club, and a confessional'.

On the site of one of Europe's first coffee houses, Venezia Trionfante (originally established in 1683), the Caffè Florian was opened in 1720 by Floriano Francesconi. During the 18th century, hot chocolate, a symbol of luxury, was the favoured drink, bitter coffee becoming more popular after the fall of the Republic.

In 1858 Ludovico Cadorin who, along with Giovanni Battista Meduna, was responsible for a revival of rococo decoration, remodelled the interior into four elegant rooms reminiscent of its 18th-century heyday. Arabs, Chinese, beautiful Moorish women and exotic Turks are depicted on the walls, and even the mirrored doors are festooned with flowers. Cadorin called the entrance Greek, the parlour Renaissance, and the coffee rooms Pompadour and Moorish, although today it is hard to pinpoint which is which. Somehow the different styles merge into a harmonious and seductive whole, termed by 19th-century critics 'Cadorin' style. It is not dissimilar to Meduna's 1854 refurbishment of La Fenice theatre.

LOCATION Piazza San Marco

VAPORETTO San Marco

ACCESS open daily, from 11.00 until midnight at least in summer, a little earlier in winter

interior Ludovico Cadorin 18th–19th centuries

CA' FARSETTI AND CA' LOREDAN

The sweep of *palazzi* on the Riva del Carbon leading up to the Rialto bridge is a powerful evocation of the early commercial importance of this area. Ca' Loredan and Ca' Farsetti are the most complete surviving examples of the earliest great merchants' houses (notwithstanding the rebuilt Fondaco dei Turchi). Ruskin considered Ca' Loredan the most beautiful palace on the Grand Canal. Ignoring the top two storeys, which are later additions, both present the wide, arcaded façades that were to set the pattern for future Venetian palace design. In both can be discerned the residual memory of flanking towers – in the raised cills at water level and, in Ca' Loredan, the two sets of paired columns at first floor. In Ca' Farsetti, however, the first-floor arcade, its arching supported on a series of delicate paired columns, is uniform across the entire façade. Behind both façades is the tripartite layout which was to become typical – at first floor a central deep grand room, at ground floor a water entrance, with storage and ancillary accommodation to either side.

The canal façade of a Venetian *palazzo* is effectively freestanding and carries no floor loading, thereby ensuring that the inevitable sinking of the façade – balanced at the water's edge – should not compromise the strength of the overall building. Over coming centuries, façade design would become increasingly open and delicate. On Ca' Loredan the marble-clad friezes contain decorative inserts, a theme – probably rooted in the spoils of war from captured Constantinople in 1204 – that would continue to develop in later centuries.

LOCATION Grand Canal/Riva del Carbon
VAPORETTO Rialto
ACCESS limited public access (offices of Venice's mayor and the city council)
VIEWPOINT Fondamenta San Silvestro (San Polo)

early 13th century

SANTO STEFANO

This early Gothic church, reminiscent of the larger monastic churches of the Frari and Santi Giovanni e Paolo, sits sideways on to the Campo Francesco Morosini, apparently because of quarrels between the Augustinians, who built the church, and neighbouring landowners. The simple three-part façade (being restored 2001), mostly brick with sharply contrasting marble spires, has a prominent portal, possibly carved by the Bon family.

Inside, there are three aisles and three apses – the central apse polygonal with Gothic windows – a 17th-century altar and attractive choir stalls. But the glory of the church is the *carena di nave* (ship's keel) roof, probably carved by Arsenale woodworkers, one of the most complex in Venice. Also notable is the painted acanthus-leaf and diamond-patterned decoration to the brick walls. Arches are framed with gilded dentillation and supported by columns of alternating white and red marble, with gilded capitals. The colour scheme is complemented by the marble floor. The decoration refers both to San Marco and the Palazzo Ducale, symbolically connecting Santo Stefano with Church and State. Important monuments include those to Giacomo Surian, probably by Pietro Lombardo (early 15th century), Doge Francesco Morosini (bronze cast by Filippo Parodi – 1694), and Senator Giovanni Falier by Antonio Canova (1801).

The campanile leans dramatically. The 16th-century cloisters are within the offices of the Ministero delle Finanze, off the Campo Sant'Angelo.

LOCATION Campiello Santo Stefano, off Campo Francesco Morosini. The Campo Sant' Angelo (cloisters) is behind, over the Rio di Sant'Angelo

VAPORETTO Accademia/San Samuele

ACCESS open Monday to Saturday, 10.00–18.00; Sunday, 15.00–18.00; cloisters open Monday to Friday, 9.00–13.00

1294–1325 (partly reconstructed in the 15th century)

SAN ZULIAN
SAN GIULIANO

Vittoria's recently restored proto-baroque façade, completed after Sansovino's death in 1570, looks like part of a dramatic stage-set only partially pulled out behind the adjacent Veneto-Byzantine building that includes the Cartier shop at its base. (Note the plaque of St George and the Dragon.) Vittoria has included not only a Latin inscription, but also Greek and Hebrew texts that praise the greatness of Tommaso Rangone, the wealthy physician from Ravenna who paid for the church to be rebuilt. His self-congratulatory likeness is carved in bronze above the portal.

This unsaintly figure outside is but a foretaste of the secular, although charming, interior. Sansovino's original plan was quite simple, probably because of the restricted site. The almost square space encloses a simple nave separated from the chancel by a vast stone arch. The chancel is formed by the central apse and two side chapels. This simplicity, however, is belied by the baroque decoration. The gilded timber ceiling (1585) with painted lunettes is complemented by the elaborate high altar by Giuseppe Sardi (1666). Noteworthy too are the stuccoes by Vittoria and a relief of the *Pietà* by Girolamo Campagna in the chapel to the left of the sanctuary, and Vittoria's statues of St Catherine of Alexandria and Daniel (south side, second altar). Take a look too at the *Pietà* by Veronese (south side, first altar).

SAN MARCO

LOCATION Campo San Zulian, off the Mercerie
VAPORETTO Rialto
ACCESS open daily, 8.45–12.00, 16.00–18.30

Jacopo Sansovino/Alessandro Vittoria rebuilt 1566

PALAZZO FALIER CANOSSA

This palace is noteworthy for its projecting covered balconies – *liagi* – forming a courtyard approach to the main façade which is set back from the water's edge. Between them is the typical central *pòrtego* with multi-light Gothic windows at *piano-nobile* level. Although restored in the 19th century, the *liagos'* basic structure is original and a rare surviving example of a common 15th-century feature, often found in Middle-Eastern architecture. However, whereas the Middle-Eastern version would have been enclosed with perforated wooden screening to prevent a view in from the street, in Venice the feature becomes also a means of display.

The Falier were an ancient Venetian family. Their first doge – Vitale Falier – was elected in 1094. He is remembered particularly for instigating the successful search for the body of St Mark, which had been lost since both San Marco and the Palazzo Ducale had been razed in a fire of 976. Some commentators also credit this family with 'discovering' the 18th-century Venetian sculptor Canova, who worked as a kitchen hand in the Falier household, and encouraging his formal studies. Certainly, his first significant work, begun aged 16 in 1773 – *Orpheus and Eurydice* (now in the Correr) – was commissioned by Giovanni Falier. Between 1861 and 1865 the American writer William Dean Howells, acting as American consul, rented rooms in the palace, subsequently publishing his work *Venetian Life*, based on the experience.

LOCATION Grand Canal/Calle Vetturi o Falier
VAPORETTO Accademia
ACCESS not open to the public
VIEWPOINT Campo dell Carità (Accademia)

early 15th century

PALAZZETTO CONTARINI-FASAN

This tiny palazzetto was, for John Ruskin, 'the richest work of the 15th-century Gothic in Venice'. He went on to say that, despite its small size, it is 'one of the principal ornaments of the very noblest reach of the Grand Canal, and would be nearly as great a loss, if it were destroyed, as the Church of La Salute itself'. It should be added that he was no great admirer of the Salute. Nevertheless this jewel-like façade is a finely balanced composition epitomising the final flowering of Venetian Gothic at a time when the transition to classical Renaissance detailing was already underway. The delicate tracery of the corbelled stone balconies, expressing motion through a wheel-like form, is unique in Venice. The whole façade is framed with twisted-rope moulding, emphasised by the stone quoining, and divided at each level by a carved cornice. At roof level intricate stone bracketing supports the final cornice. Windows – a trio at first floor and separate single openings at second – are framed with delicate stone columns and capitals from which the traditional ogee Gothic arch springs, to be topped by a sumptuous florid finial. Each element – solid or void, coloured brickwork or white stone, textured carving or flat plane – works within a harmonious and symmetrical whole. Although now remodelled, the lower level would have originally incorporated the traditional watergate.

LOCATION Grand Canal
VAPORETTO Salute for the viewpoint
ACCESS not open to the public
VIEWPOINT Campo della Salute (Dorsoduro)

C 1475

PALAZZO LANDO-CORNER-SPINELLI

This building precisely captures that moment of stylistic transition between Gothic and Renaissance Venetian palace architecture. Codussi has taken the florid form of Gothic seen at, for instance, Ca' d'Oro, and combined this with earlier Veneto-Byzantine forms to produce a uniquely Venetian solution. The façade is tightly organised – symmetrical, framed with classical pilasters and topped with a swagged frieze. Traditional decorative coloured marble roundels are incorporated but precisely laid out. As is typical, the window disposition reflects the accommodation behind – a central main space, lit by the paired openings – with flanking wings. However, the window form is unprecedented – paired windows, with a central oculus over, all enclosed within a single arch.

Balustrading at both first- and second-floor levels orders and enlivens the façade, but again a note of Gothic breaks through in the unique use of three-section balustrading to either side at first-floor level. The whole rises above rusticated Istrian ground-floor and mezzanine walling, which recalls Codussi's earlier innovation at the church of San Michele in Isola. Such solid rustication – later almost universally adopted – is a clear architectural indicator that merchants were now less likely to store goods on the lower floors of their own houses, but would keep them in centralised warehouses around the Rialto – reducing the need for a large goods water gate. All these elements can be seen developed to even greater refinement in the Palazzo Loredan-Vendramin-Calergi.

LOCATION Grand Canal/Campiello del Teatro
VAPORETTO Sant'Angelo
ACCESS not open to the public
VIEWPOINT Calle del Traghetto della Madonnetta (San Polo)

Mauro Codussi 1490–1510

SCALA CONTARINI 'DEL BOVOLO'

There's nothing like this extraordinary spiral staircase (*bovolo* is Venetian dialect for 'snail') anywhere else in the city. While it is a stunning architectural achievement in itself, it appears to have been stuck on to the now-dilapidated late-Gothic palace behind with casual bravado – particularly on the left-hand side. On the right the staircase is linked to the main building with loggias in a similar style, allowing easy access to palace rooms while creating a typically asymmetrical Venetian façade.

In the 'bovolo', Candi has blended early Renaissance elements with Byzantine and Gothic techniques in the traditionally Venetian manner, which creates a pleasing whole out of mix-and-match features. This is despite the fact that the arches of the spiral are not regular and the whole building is out-of-scale with the streetscape below.

The brick façade is liberally laced with Istrian stone balustrades, arches and supporting columns, which are both light in touch and important for the structural stability of the staircase. The arches of both the loggias and the staircase decrease in height on the upper storeys. The circular cupola at the top is made of lead. Older mosaics are still visible behind the brick as you climb the staircase to catch a wonderful view of the city. You can pick out almost every belltower, with good views of San Marco, Santa Maria della Salute and San Giorgio Maggiore as well as the top of the campanile of Santo Stefano.

Outside is a little garden with a display of seven wellheads.

LOCATION Corte dei Risi o del Bovolo
VAPORETTO San Marco or Rialto
ACCESS open daily, April to October, 10.30–17.30.
May be open later in the year – check at the tourist office

Giovanni Candi c 1499

FONDACO DEI TEDESCHI

The merchant trading post, *fondaco*, was a building type common along the trade routes to the East. Typically rented from the local ruling authority, it would be both a focus for a foreign community and a point of import and distribution of a particular country's goods. Venice itself would have maintained such facilities throughout the Byzantine empire.

A Fondaco dei Tedeschi had been established on this site from the 13th century, providing a trade outlet for northern-European merchants. In 1505 this burnt down, and it is a reflection of the importance of this trade that the Republic required it to be reconstructed within three years. Built by Spavento, to a concept by Gerolamo Tedesco, it is centred around an open court – retailing and goods storage at the lower levels, meeting rooms and accommodation for visiting traders above. The central courtyard, now gloomy under its translucent roof covering, is a subtle composition of diminishing open arcades.

Designed as a strictly functional facility, its façades today appear austere, the only reference to more familiar forms of architectural treatment being the five-arched loading portico, possibly by Scarpagnino. When first built, however, the Republic, rejecting architectural decoration, commissioned Titian and Giorgione to fresco the outside walls (fragments are now in the Accademia). On the Grand Canal today, only the mosaics of the Casa Salviati and the Palazzo Barberigo demonstrate this decorative approach.

LOCATION Fontego dei Tedeschi
VAPORETTO Rialto
ACCESS open commercial hours –- this is now the central post office
VIEWPOINT Rialto bridge

Gerolamo Tedesco (concept), Giorgio Spavento and Scarpagnino 1505–08

PALAZZO CORNER DELLA CA' GRANDE

Dubbed by Vasari as 'perhaps the most splendid residence in Italy', but by Ruskin as 'one of the worst and coldest buildings of the central Renaissance', the Ca' Grande is a benchmark for the Roman-style palazzo which was to dominate High-Renaissance Venetian design. It was commissioned by the Corner family, who were both fabulously wealthy – partly through their relation by marriage to the King of Cyprus – and also well connected to Roman society. Sansovino adopts elements familiar from Roman and Tuscan architecture – oval attic windows with scrolled framing, voluted corbels to ground-floor and mezzanine windows – but works them into a Venetian design. For instance, the seven windows at upper levels, while separated by paired classical columns, create a virtual arcade in the Venetian tradition. At the same time, such regularity departs from the previous tradition of windows reflecting the use behind – there is almost no differentiation between the central windows lighting the upper-level central reception spaces and those of the flanking wings. Gone also are the traditional marble inserts retained in early Renaissance work at, for example, Codussi's Palazzos Lando-Corner-Spinelli and Loredan-Vendramin-Calergi. The rusticated base, balustrading and paired columns are now resolved into an even tighter overall compostion. Stylistically, the design is also reminiscent of Sansovino's public work on the Marciana Library – perhaps no coincidence for a family that blurred the boundaries between State and individual power.

LOCATION Grand Canal/Fondamenta Corner-Zaguri
VAPORETTO Santa Maria Del Giglio
ACCESS limited public access (offices of the State Prefecture)
VIEWPOINT Palazzo Venier dei Leoni (Guggenheim Museum), Dorsoduro

Jacopo Sansovino 1537–81

PALAZZO GRIMANI

Palazzo Grimani is designed on the most heroic scale, dwarfing its neighbours with a façade that epitomises the High Renaissance in Venice. Even Ruskin was lavish in his praise, calling it the noblest Venetian building to have been constructed since the Palazzo Ducale. Sanmicheli has drawn on precedents from Codussi's Palazzo Loredan-Vendramin-Calergi – the illusion of uniformity in storey height, the strong horizontal cornicing – and Sansovino's Palazzo Corner della Ca' Grande, to produce an innovative façade based on the classical form of the Roman triumphal arch. Its overriding design motif is the so-called Serlian window form – a central arched opening flanked by lesser, square-headed openings. This form was first documented in 1537 by Sebastiano Serlio – a refugee from the Sack of Rome. Sanmicheli uses it as a development of the traditional Venetian central multi-light window. At water level, three central arches front a square atrium divided by rows of paired columns. The façade detailing is highly modelled – the strong grid of Corinthian columns and entablatures forming a massive framework which barely hints at the traditional tripartite layout of spaces behind. Symbolically, this building would have reinforced the Venetian belief that, following Rome's fall in 1527, the mantle of Roman power and splendour had naturally passed to Venice.

Sanmicheli died in 1559, when the *piano nobile* was barely started, and building work was completed by Giangiacomo de' Grigi and Antonio Rusconi.

LOCATION Grand Canal/Calle Grimani
VAPORETTO Rialto
ACCESS limited (the building now houses the law courts)
VIEWPOINT Calle Barzizza (San Polo)

Michele Sanmicheli 1556–75

SAN GIORGIO MAGGIORE MONASTERY AND CLOISTERS
CINI FOUNDATION

Benedictine monks first settled on this small island in 982, and for many centuries the monastery was one of great political importance. Cosimo de' Medici, banished from Florence in 1433, fled behind its doors, bringing with him Michelozzo, architect of the first, now-demolished, library. The doge and his entourage visited on St Stephen's Day every year, and in 1800 the papal court took up residence in the monastery to escape the French.

Jacopo de' Barbari's map of Venice (1500) shows the older Gothic buildings and gardens quite clearly. None of these is visible today, but in their place is a collection of architectural wonders, including a cloister and refectory by Palladio, and a grand staircase and reading room by Longhena. The monks still live and work here, and their robed figures ambling through the cloisters add an authentic touch of medieval scholasticism. In 1951 the monastery was taken over by the art patron, Count Vittorio Cini, who named it after his son Giorgio. As a result, the monastery now houses collections of paintings and furniture, and hosts conferences and courses in the arts.

In 1560 the monks asked Palladio to redesign the existing refectory (now also called the Cenacolo Palladiano). It is reached from his cloister (see below), where the gallery acts as a processional walkway to the refectory complex. This is cool and uniform, with door and window surrounds in the same palette as the stuccoed elevations. The ceiling of the hall and two anterooms are at the same height, so the lower rooms are imposingly high and lead visually to the main hall. The latter, a beautifully proportioned room, has a barrel roof with one vault in the middle, bringing the eye upwards at this point. Palladio's three grand windows penetrating the vault are now blocked.

The two sets of cloisters are similar in size but different in feel. Giovanni Buora's Cloister of the Cypresses, begun in 1517, with its paired Veneto-Byzantine windows over wide arches, and with a central wellhead decorated with swags of fruits and a female fig-

Giovanni Buora, Baldassare Longhena, Andrea Palladio 16th–17th centuries

SAN GIORGIO MAGGIORE MONASTERY AND CLOISTERS

ure, harks back to an earlier style, while Palladio's Cloister of the Bay Trees (1579, well after his work on the church [page 5.46] and completed in the mid 17th century, long after his death in 1580) is more like the state buildings of Sansovino's Procuratie Vecchie in appearance than Palladio's other cloister at the Carità. Because of this, Palladio's authorship of the San Giorgio cloisters was under question until the plans were found among his possessions many years later. Longhena may have designed the open loggia between the two cloisters.

Up Longhena's grand staircase, the star turn is his beautifully restored library, housing more than 100,000 books. The wooden book cupboards, topped with carved figures and set off with fluted columns and Ionic capitals, are separated by tall arched windows. The roof is barrel-vaulted and contains five carved insets for paintings. Over the side door are the words *Balthasar Longhena architectus Venetus*. Also on this level is Giovanni Buora's long dormitory (c 1494).

The monastery gardens lead past the Teatro Verde, an amphitheatre designed by Luigi Vietti and Angelo Scattolin in 1952, using material found on the island during the restoration of its buildings. The steps are in white Vicenza stone interposed with box hedging for seat backs. The stage covers 1400 square metres. The construction of this theatre necessitated reclaiming the marshy terrain and building a waterproof foundation – a traditional Venetian problem with an elegant solution.

LOCATION Isola di San Giorgio Maggiore (access only by boat)
VAPORETTO Isola San Giorgio
ACCESS by appointment only. Call in at the secretary's office by the main gate

Giovanni Buora, Baldassare Longhena, Andrea Palladio 16th–17th centuries

SAN GIORGIO MAGGIORE

From the Piazza San Marco, the façade of San Giorgio (commissioned in 1565 to replace a Gothic predecessor, and completed after Palladio's death by Simone Sorella) beckons like the gateway to a heavenly city: the two superimposed Istrian stone temples glistening in the sun and rippling in watery reflections. The simple structure is a development of Palladio's design of San Francesco della Vigna. When commissioned by the Benedictines to design the church, he had already designed the monastery's refectory (see page 5.42).

The cool interior of white Istrian stone and stucco is flooded with light from the high-level windows, an effect inspired by the design of Roman baths. The Greek/Latin cross hybrid plan allowed Palladio to allude to Vitruvius while providing for the ecclesiastical requirements of the Benedictines.The interior mimics the façade in its use of major and minor orders (a Palladian innovation), the high pedestals and columns dwarfing mere humans in the presence of the divine. On the high altar by Aliense, Girolamo Campagna's beautifully executed 17th-century bronze sculpture of Christ on a globe supported by the Evangelists and flanked by a pair of angels by Pietro Boselli, is secular by comparison.

The monks still gather in the elegant choir stalls behind the altar, their singing enveloping the congregation and charging the atmosphere, bringing extra drama to Tintoretto's *Last Supper* and the *Shower of Manna*, on the walls of the chancel.

Climb Scalfarotto's campanile (1729) for a great view of the Piazza San Marco and the San Giorgio Maggiore monastery and cloisters.

LOCATION Isola di San Giorgio Maggiore
VAPORETTO San Giorgio Maggiore
ACCESS open daily, 10.00–12.30, 15.00–16.30

Andrea Palladio 1566–1611

SAN MOISÈ

Adjacent to the modernist Hotel Bauer-Grünwald, the baroque façade of San Moisè (called by Ruskin 'one of the basest examples of the basest schools of the Renaissance') is its almost comical counterpart. Along with the Scalzi, Santa Maria del Giglio and Ospedaletto façades, however, San Moisè is indicative of the 17th-century baroque fashion for integrating sculpture with architecture, bringing a new interest to Renaissance geometry. It is also a fulsome example of self-glorification (in this case of the Fini family), which in earlier centuries had been more usually restricted to interior church sculpture. The Fini paid for the reconstruction of this medieval church, which was already a remodelling – there has been a church on this spot since the 7th century.

Tremignon's tripartite façade was decorated by the Flemish sculptor Heinrich Meyring to honour Vincenzo Fini, made Procurator of San Marco in 1687. His bust on the central obelisk (the camels may refer to the family's trading links with the Levant) is flanked by two other family busts. The Fini coat of arms is over the main doorway. Saints, columns, festoons and imaginary animals complete the bizarre scene. The bell tower is 14th century.

The interior, with a simple nave, main chapel and two side chapels, is dominated by Meyring's rocky narrative sculpture on the high altar (1684), showing God handing the tablets to Moses, all backed with an integral fresco. Below is Meyring's *Adoration of the Golden Calf*.

LOCATION Campo San Moisè
VAPORETTO San Marco
ACCESS open daily, 15.30–19.00

Alessandro Tremignon/Heinrich (Enrico) Meyring 1668

SANTA MARIA DEL GIGLIO
SANTA MARIA ZOBENIGO

Although more refined in its decoration than the façade of San Moisè, this façade is another example of a full-blown baroque family monument, completely rebuilt in the 17th century by a follower of Longhena, Giuseppe Sardi. A donation of 30,000 ducats from Antonio Barbaro, a member of an important military and sea-faring family who had held office for the Serenissima in foreign outposts, financed the project. Barbaro commissioned Sardi to follow a strict iconographical programme, which included a life-size statue of himself in the full regalia of a sea captain, flanked by allegorical figures, and of his brothers – all sculpted by Juste Le Court. These curly-wigged characters stand in niches usually peopled with saints; religious fervour is notable by its absence. At the top, the curvilinear pediment frames the family coat of arms. Below the lower order are carved views of the cities where Antonio held office. Angels, leaning out over this strongly three-dimensional façade into the *campo*, trumpet the family's importance. We are left in no doubt as to the Barbaro family's opinion of itself.

Attached to a much-restructured 10th-century church named after the the lily (*giglio*) that the angel Gabriel gave to the Virgin Mary, and the local Jubanico (Zobenigo) family, this façade was Sardi's last work and has much in common with his Scalzi church – note the double order of twinned columns.

In 1775 the 13th-century campanile fell down and was never replaced.

LOCATION Campo Santa Maria Zobenigo
VAPORETTO San Marco
ACCESS open Monday to Saturday, 10.00–18.00, Sunday, 15.00–18.00

Giuseppe Sardi 1680–83

PALAZZO GRASSI

It is easy to miss Palazzo Grassi; its understated neoclassical style is all but overwhelmed by the grandiose Ca' Rezzonico on the opposite bank. However, its design, patronage and date of construction mark it out as significant – it is the last great palace to be built in Venice. Designed by Massari, the architect who completed the Ca' Rezzonico, its rather severe interpretation of classical design owes much to the work of Sansovino's Palazzo Corner della Ca' Grande, built two centuries earlier. This reversion to the Roman precedent – so important in self-aggrandising 16th-century Venice – ironically now occurs in the twilight years of a Republic which would shortly fall to Napoleon's invasion. The building's patron – the Grassi family – had relatively recently joined the ranks of Venice's patricians through its generous donations to the Republic's wars against the Turks in 1718. Such *arrivistes* were increasingly common as Venice's power and wealth declined. By the time the Republic finally fell, the Grassi were one of its richest families.

The palace's plan is as formal as its façade: it is centred on an internal courtyard reminiscent of Sansovino's work in the Roman tradition. Unusually, there is a public side elevation facing on to Campo San Samuele and, owing to its recent restoration by its current owners – the Agnelli family of Fiat fame – it is frequently open to the public as an exhibition space. The restoration work was undertaken by Antonio Foscari and Gae Aulenti (architect of the Musee d'Orsay conversion in Paris).

LOCATION Grand Canal/Campo San Samuele
VAPORETTO San Samuele
ACCESS public access during exhibitions
VIEWPOINT Calle Bernardo (Dorsoduro)

Giorgio Massari 1748–72/Antonio Foscari and Gae Aulenti (20th-century restoration)

SAN MAURIZIO

Gianantonio Selva, the neoclassical architect responsible for creating the Via Garibaldi, the entrance to the Giardini Pubblici (1810) and, more famously, the Fenice theatre (begun 1790 – now under reconstruction after being almost totally destroyed by fire in 1997), was a writer-historian, and a pupil of another neoclassical devotee, Tommaso Temanza. For the 19th-century reconstruction of San Maurizio, rebuilt to look like San Germiniano, the church destroyed by Napoleon to provide space for the Ala Napoleonica in Piazza San Marco, Selva joined forces with Antonio Diedo.

The church's origins are 11th century, and its first transformation had been in 1580 when it was reoriented to overlook this charming *campo*, not far from the Piazza San Marco. Today's severe, purist façade is entirely of Istrian stone, lightened by the lively bas-relief of the triangular pediment, depicting scenes from the life of the soldier and martyr, St Maurice. Two other bas-relief panels sit symmetrically on either side of the semicircular window. The Ionic doorway and lower windows have a tomb-like gloom about them, but the scholarly attention to neoclassical detail cannot be denied.

The interior is a Greek-cross plan and is simple rather than stark, not unlike the work of that master of the early Renaissance, Mauro Codussi.

Consecrated in 1828, the church is now deconsecrated and only occasionally used for public exhibitions and other non-religious purposes.

LOCATION Campo San Maurizio, on the main drag between the Piazza San Marco and the Accademia bridge
VAPORETTO Santa Maria del Giglio
ACCESS open only for occasional exhibitions

Gianantonio Selva and Antonio Diedo rebuilt 1806

COFFEE HOUSE

Architectural and symbolic expression of Venice's fall to Napoleon can be most clearly seen concentrated around the Republic's administrative heart in San Marco. Following plans by Giovanni Antolini, Napoleon's intent was to reconstruct the western end of the piazza and create a royal palace within the Procuratie Nuove, whose southern frontage would look directly out over the Grand Canal. The first goal was realised through the creation of the Ala Napoleonica. As to the second, the intended vista was created through the demolition of vast medieval granaries which stood on the site of today's Giardini ex Reali. But the proposals for a new southern façade were never enacted and today the chief architectural record of the ambitions for the site is this small neoclassical pavilion by Lorenzo Santi.

Constructed throughout in Istrian stone with rusticated lower storey and a central dome raised on a rusticated drum, it was conceived as a coffee house. Some critics have focused on its awkward scale – the deep, swagged upper frieze and extraordinary corner urns seeming to overburden the diminutive Doric colonnade and frieze below. In contrast with the exuberant confection of its external detailing, the interior presents a cool, finely drawn composition, calming the general chaos associated with its current function as the city's main tourist information office.

LOCATION Il Molo (adjoining Giardini ex Reali)
VAPORETTO San Marco
ACCESS open Monday to Saturday, 9.40–15.20

Lorenzo Santi 1815–17

ART NOUVEAU SHOP SIGN

Guarding his corner between San Marco and the Ponte di Rialto, this ferocious, wrought-iron dragon/bird, with huge claws, aggressively folded wings, spiky neck and a glare that transfixes the eye, carries his harmless and colourful prey: three glass umbrellas which at night cast a jolly glow over the *calle* here. Although the shop it protects now sells leather goods, it was once chiefly an outlet for umbrellas.

Stylistically such wrought-iron work is linked to the Venetian version of art nouveau seen in buildings such as the Villa Hérriot, the commercial building in the Bacino Orseolo and the many idiosyncratic buildings on the Lido.

LOCATION on the corner of Merceria II Aprile and the Merceria San Salvador, very near the Ponte di Rialto
VAPORETTO Rialto

early 1900s

COMMERCIAL BUILDING, BACINO ORSEOLO

An example of Venetian art nouveau, this building is by the architect who built the rather more exotic Villa Monplaisir on the Lido two years earlier. From a distance it may be difficult to see the particular period charm of this multi-storey building, as the art-nouveau detailing is more subtle than that of the villa and the geometric volume of sterner stuff. Get closer, however, and you see the gently undulating lower balconies with delicate wrought-iron decoration, and the similarly shaped stone balconies to the upper level. Just under the stone-bracketed overhanging roof a painted frieze with stone roundel inserts is all that remains of the original secessionist art-nouveau decoration that covered the upper storeys. Less successful are the strange composite Ionic/Byzantine column capitals compressed into the stone-dressed windows on the *piano nobile*, in imitation of traditional Veneto-Byzantine palazzo detailing. Stone cut-outs and quoining to the façades further echo memories of traditional Istrian stone detailing. At roof level a starkly rectilinear enclosed version of the traditional Venetian *altana* rises alongside a dramatically curved arched dormer window. To the side façade a stone-dressed doorway adopts a more neoclassical styling, relieved, however, by florid decorative wrought ironwork.

This is a building that rewards closer study. In the best tradition of Venetian architecture, Sullam has sought to evolve a contemporary style – drawing on broader architectural development but rooted in the traditions of the city's architecture – to create something uniquely Venetian.

LOCATION Fondamenta Orseolo, near Piazza San Marco
VAPORETTO San Marco
ACCESS not open to the public

Guido Costante Sullam 1908–10

NARDI'S HOUSING

This early-20th-century development, commissioned by the Nardi family, dominates the courtyard leading away from the Sant'Angelo *vaporetto* stop. Its style is full-blown Veneto-Byzantine revivalist – a technical *tour de force* incorporating design elements culled from Venice's 13th–15th century palaces. Although at first sight it looks like a vast palazzo, it was in fact built speculatively as an apartment block. Predominately of brick with decorative detailing, it incorporates stone cills, padstones and columns within the multi-light windows. Included within a series of stone and marble insert panels is one, at third-floor level, that records the names of those involved in its design and construction. The style of this panel is borrowed from the traditional portrayal of members of a confraternity sheltering in the protection of their patron saint, here secularised to portray the patron and artisan.

Rather than integrating with its neighbouring buildings, its sheer scale redefines the immediate area and, in common with a number of other 20th-century redevelopments (for example, the nearby Cassa di Risparmio) it has accordingly been much criticised.

SAN MARCO

LOCATION Corte dell' Albero
VAPORETTO Sant'Angelo
ACCESS not open to the public

Giulio Alessandri 1909–14

BAUER-GRÜNWALD HOTEL

It would be hard to find a building with a worse press than the 1940s wing of this hotel flanking the baroque façade of San Moisè (other than, perhaps, San Moisè itself).

Originally an 18th-century palazzo, it was opened as a hotel in 1880 by two Austrians, Mr Bauer and Julius Grünwald. Its foreign provenance may well explain some of the vitriol its subsequent rebuilding attracted. During the 1940s, Bennati commissioned a neo-Gothic makeover for the hotel's former 18th-century Grand Canal façade and, at the same time, added the wing that now fronts the Campo di San Moisè and also presents a second façade to the Canal. Seen from the *campo*, the modern movement façade may be at odds with the surrounding buildings, but it undoubtedly follows Venetian palazzo tradition in its composition – the large surface area of void compared to solid, the traditional run of small windows on the top storey, and the grand open ground-floor entrance. It is, admittedly, more difficult to admire the stripped-back style of its Grand Canal frontage abutting the neo-Gothic façade.

Inside, beyond the reception space, is a spectacular 1940s ballroom with mirrored walls and cascading pink lights, wonderfully evocative of its era. Most recently, in 1999, a further internal refurbishment was completed, intended to reinforce the two distinctly different styles at work in this building.

Some scenes in *The Talented Mr Ripley* (Anthony Minghella, 1998) were filmed here. To enjoy a view from the highest outdoor terrace in Venice, take the lift to the Settimo Cielo bar.

LOCATION Campo San Moisè
VAPORETTO San Marco
ACCESS general access to public areas

17th–20th centuries, new wing M Meo 1949–54

OLIVETTI SHOWROOM

For many, Scarpa's best-known Venetian work is this masterly creation within one of the ground-floor units of the Procuratie Vecchie. Originally commissioned by art patron Adriano Olivetti for his company's showroom, its appearance today initially seems overwhelmed by the clutter of its current retail use. Beware also of the shop staff, long grown weary of the impecunious architectural-design devotee.

Outside, the work announces its presence through a neutral palette of dressed and rough stonework and metal, inserted into the original structure of the Procuratie Vecchie, housing, to the side, a stone pivoted door and, to the front, a gridded metal main entrance guarded by two timber-screened mezzanine-level windows.

Central to the restructuring of the interior is the magnificent staircase of Aurisina stone, its treads apparently floating up to the first-floor gallery from the water-like Murano-glass-tiled floor surface. The riserless steps extend into, and interact with, adjacent slabs of stone like a reassembly of more ancient blocks of structural stonework. In every element within the galleries there is meticulous attention to detail in the delicate, but always robust, use of timber and metal.

Scarpa's respect for, and understanding of, good craftsmanship continues in the great tradition of Venetian architecture and has produced a work that is both sensitive to its historical context and entirely forward looking. (see the Palazzo Querini-Stampalia, the galleries in the Cà d'Oro, the University entrance at the Tolentini and at San Sebastiano).

LOCATION north side of the Piazza San Marco (arcade of the Procuratie Vecchie)
VAPORETTO San Marco
ACCESS open during shop hours – ask permission from the shopkeeper to look around

Carlo Scarpa 1957–58

CASSA DI RISPARMIO

Optimistically anticipated before its construction as a building capable of positively trans-forming Campo Manin, the reality is that the Cassa di Risparmio has attracted its fair share of criticism. Structurally innovative in order to cope with the specific ground condi-tions – it is founded on only four columns and incorporates a massive transfer beam at second-floor level – the building's scale inevitably overwhelms the space around it. Its detailing and use of materials, however, is impeccable and incorporates explicit refer-ences to the Venetian architectural tradition – for example, the double order of upper-level windows with recessed sections reminiscent of loggias and the green glass undercill panels recalling the marble *paterae* of historic palazzi. Based on a foundation of Istrian stone, a ground level of stone panels, massively bolted into place, is broken only by the public entrances to this bank building. Above – hanging from the second-floor structure – a storey of curtain-wall glazing emphasises the 'solid' upper levels, inverting the tradi-tional structural form. The whole is topped by two glazed gabled roofs rising behind the rectilinear façade.

In the 30 years since completion of the Cassa di Risparmio it is perhaps significant that no one has been granted permission to put up a new commercial development in the historic centre.

LOCATION Campo Manin
VAPORETTO Rialto
ACCESS open during commercial hours

Angelo Scattolin/Pier Luigi Nervi (engineer) 1964–71

BRONZEWORK ON THE TEATRO GOLDONI

There has been a theatre on this site since 1622 when the building was owned by the Vendramin family, but it has been rebuilt many times since then and was only named after the playwright Carlo Goldoni, sometimes called the Venetian Molière, in 1875.

Closed during the post-war period because it was dangerously unstable, the theatre was compulsorily purchased by the State in 1957 when it underwent a long and thorough restoration, bringing it firmly into the 20th century.

Today, its chief contribution to the richness of Venetian street architecture is its series of bronze panels and doors depicting aspects of Venetian life. The façade, wth stone doorsets, steps and window surrounds, dates from 1979, when Gianni Arico's bronze panels were completed. The balcony plaques show Venetian buildings, including San Giacometto, San Stae, San Marco and the Cannaregio bridge. The figure of Goldoni lurks on the right-hand door among a host of theatrical characters. On the left-hand door is a representation of Santa Maria della Salute during the traditional festival of the marriage with the sea. The centre door panels are devoted to 'Le Arti' and 'Il Teatro'.

Goldoni is immortalised in a sculpture, cast in bronze by Dal Zotto in 1883, and located in the Campo San Bartolomeo near the Rialto bridge.

LOCATION Calle del Teatro, Rialto
VAPORETTO Rialto
ACCESS exterior always viewable; interior open for performances

Gianni Arico restored 1979

SAN POLO

SAN GIACOMETTO
SAN GIACOMO DI RIALTO

Supposedly dating from 421, and possibly the oldest church in Venice, San Giacometto is sometimes attributed to the Cretan architect, Entinopos. It is the much-loved and atmospheric hub of the market square established here, probably in the 11th century. For a long time this square was as crucial to Venice's commercial activities as the Piazza San Marco was to its government and every year on Ash Wednesday and Good Friday the doge visited the church. Restored around 1071, the earliest reliable documentation dates from 1152.

The 15th-century porch (restored 1958), which once sheltered bankers and money changers, is one of only two left in the city (the other is at San Nicolò dei Mendicoli). Its roof is supported by five columns on octagonal bases with richly ornamented foliate capitals. Dominating the façade like a benevolent smiling face is the huge, hopelessly inaccurate, 15th-century clock. The jaunty doorway, striped in red Verona marble and white Istrian stone, has dentilled ornamentation, a Moorish feature. Above the clock, three bells sit in their pedimented surrounds.

Six ancient Greek marble columns with 11th-century Corinthian capitals enliven the interior – a small Greek-cross plan with a dome over the transept – which may have been a model for San Marco. A 16th-century restoration opened up the semicircular windows and destroyed some vivid mosaics, but retained the layout. The high altar (early 17th century) was designed by Scamozzi; the statue of St Anthony Abbot is by Girolamo Campagna.

LOCATION Campo San Giacomo. The Santa Croce side of the Rialto bridge, off the Ruga degli Orefici
VAPORETTO Rialto
ACCESS open daily, 9.00–12.00, 16.00–18.00

12th century

SANTA MARIA GLORIOSA DEI FRARI
I FRARI

Generally known as I Frari (The Brothers), this Franciscan church is one of two great Gothic churches in Venice (see also Santi Giovanni e Paolo in Castello). At first sight austere, its simple beauty can be seen from the *campo* at its north-eastern front, where *oculi* lead the eye back through three receding planes of doorways. Alternatively, approached from the Campo di San Rocco, its traceried Gothic apse dominates that otherwise Renaissance square and was noted by Ruskin as being the 'real root' of the Palazzo Ducale, since the design of its stonework mouldings was directly adapted for that building's great arcade.

The Frari defies liturgical convention because its apse faces south-west, allowing afternoon sunlight to flood into the chancel where visitors now enter. It is a building of brick-vaulted ceilings – a rare feature in Venice due to understandable concern that differential settlement could easily cause collapse; hence the gridding of timber tie beams. The exposed internal brickwork is not quite what it seems – it is painted over, a common medieval Venetian building practice intended to beautify, regularise and refine an otherwise humble material.

Between the nave and the chancel stands the enclosed choir (1460–75), separated from the main body by a richly decorated marble screen, generally thought to be the work of Pietro Lombardo. The choir stalls within are particularly fine, Marco Cozzi's marquetry panels showing a series of views of the 'ideal city'. Monumental tombs surround the nave. Antonio Rizzo's tomb of Doge Nicolò Tron (c 1476) rates as the most imposing of Venice's 15th-century funerary monuments. That to Doge Giovanni Pesaro, designed by Baldassare Longhena (1669), is a baroque *tour de force*, comprising four vast Moors (representing defeated Turks) shouldering a panoply of allegorical figures surrounding the doge himself, enthroned under a canopy of red marble 'brocade'. Perhaps unsurprisingly it was not appreciated by Ruskin. Nor was the adjoining pyramidal tomb to Canova – 'consumate

Baldassare Longhena, Jacopo Sansovino, Marco Cozzi, and others 14th–15th centuries

6.6

in science, intolerable in affectation, ridiculous in conception, null and void to the uttermost in invention and feeling'. Both raise questions of the relationship between temporal and religious power in the Serenissima.

To the far left of the chancel is the Corner chapel (1417), an early example of the extensive patronage of wealthy Venetians, in this case, the Corner family (see also the Cappella Cornaro, Cannaregio). Retaining its 15th-century glazing, it is dedicated to St Mark and contains Jacopo Sansovino's late sculptural masterpiece of *St John the Baptist* (1560) which can be contrasted with the extraordinary wooden statue of the same subject by Donatello (1438) in the chapel immediately to the right of the chancel. The chapel also contains a luminous Vivarini tryptych of an enthroned St Mark (1474). To the far right is the sacristy which still contains Giovanni Bellini's *Madonna and Child* tryptych (1488). Mounted on the right-hand wall is a touching 14th-century tablet showing the Virgin sheltering brothers under her cloak. Two cloisters – the 17th-century Cloister of the Holy Trinity, and the earlier Cloister of St Anthony, designed by the school of Sansovino – now house the state archives and, at the time of writing, are regrettably closed to visitors without authority to enter the archives.

SAN POLO

LOCATION Campo dei Frari
VAPORETTO San Tomà
ACCESS open 9.30–12.00, 14.20-18.00; closed Sunday

Baldassare Longhena, Jacopo Sansovino, Marco Cozzi, and others 14th–15th centuries

SCUOLA GRANDE DI SAN GIOVANNI EVANGELISTA

One of the oldest and richest of Venetian *scuole grandi* (see Introduction, page 0.11–0.14), and a great rival of the Scuola Grande di San Marco, this establishment gained huge prestige and large cash donations when it obtained a relic of the Holy Cross in 1369 – a fact commemorated in Gentile Bellini's late-15th-century paintings, now in the Accademia. In 1414, the *scuola* acquired this site from the Badoer family, and building work started.

With its growing importance, the *scuola* employed Mauro Codussi and Pietro Lombardo to ratify its position in Venetian society and, in terms of the code of *scuole grandi*, giving due reverence to its holy relic. Lombardo's beautifully carved portal screen to the courtyard (1481) and Codussi's *scuola* portal and grand double staircase (1498), commissioned after his work on the Scuola di San Marco staircase, are the principal attractions. Some of the bas-reliefs on the screen (for example, the angels at the top) may have been by Tullio Lombardo (Pietro's son) but the decorative frieze above and the marble facing and disc decoration are typical of Pietro's work and reminiscent of Santa Maria dei Miracoli. The eagle above the portal is a symbol of the Evangelist. On the entrance façade is a 14th-century sculpture, relocated from a previous building, showing members of the *scuola* kneeling before the Evangelist.

The upper chapter hall, overhauled in 1720 by Giorgio Massari, compares unfavourably with the simple columned *androne*, or lower hall, and the attractively restored *campiello*.

LOCATION north of the Campo dei Frari. Take Rio Terrà San Tomà and Calle Magazèn
VAPORETTO San Tomà
ACCESS interior open for public meetings and concerts. Check at the tourist office

Mauro Codussi/Pietro Lombardo 1414–1512

DIVO IOANNI APOSTOLO ET EVANGELISTAE
PROTECTORI ET SANCTISSIMAE CRVCI

SCUOLA DEI CALEGHERI

Whereas some of the smaller *scuole* were formed to protect particular nationality groups (for example, the Scuola di San Giovanni degli Schiavoni, the Dalmatians), others were formed as registered guilds (known as *arti*) for trades or crafts. The Arsenale ropemakers were the first to be registered in 1233, and eventually each Venetian trade or craft was represented by its own guild. These guilds enforced quality control, ensured training standards, and, like the larger *scuole*, looked after members and their families. They were also an important source of patronage for artists and sculptors.

Most trade guild halls were modest and functional (indeed some guilds had no building at all). The late-Gothic Scuola dei Calegheri (shoemakers – sometimes written in Venetian dialect, *Calzolai*) is one of the oldest to survive. On its façade are two bas-reliefs: one, a common image in Venice (see, for example, the façade of the Scuola Grande di San Giovanni Evangelista), shows the guild members kneeling in prayer under the protective cloak of the Virgin. Above the doorway is a charming work, probably by Antonio Rizzo (1478), of St Mark healing Anianus the Shoemaker. The little guild thus proudly displays its relationship to the Scuola Grande di San Marco, where two carvings of Anianus by Tullio Lombardo grace the façade, at the same time giving status to the city's artisans and honouring the powers of its patron saint.

LOCATION Campo San Tomà, opposite the church
VAPORETTO San Tomà
ACCESS not open to the public

Antonio Rizzo (sculptor) 1478

SCUOLA GRANDE DI SAN ROCCO

This important *scuola* – home to Venice's wealthiest confraternity, owing to their patron saint's alleged power to cure plague – epitomises the tension between the charitable principles of a *scuola*'s foundation and the ambitions of its membership. The original building of the 1490s, standing opposite in the shadow of the austere brick Frari, had been quickly outgrown. Bartolomeo Bon's design for its successor owed much to Codussi – for example the paired windows with *oculi* first seen at Palazzo Lando-Corner-Spinelli. However, Bon was sacked in 1524, with construction barely above first-floor level. Sante Lombardo designed the upper rear canal façade before he was sacked in 1527. Next came Scarpagnino, whose heavily worked orders of Corinthian columns now dominate the main façade.

The building's use is easily read – three bays defining the grand assembly spaces with, to the right, two subsidiary bays corresponding to today's entrance, and, at first-floor level, the governing body's small meeting room or *albergo*. The imposing internal staircase – an innovative design by Scarpagnino – belies its stormy creation. Bon was sacked for refusing to implement Giovanni Celestro's original design (chosen from several, including one by the snubbed Bon). Sante Lombardo therefore began it, and it was completed by Scarpagnino. In the end the *scuola*'s elders pronounced it unsuitable. It was demolished and Scarpagnino designed the current staircase. It leads to the grandest of first-floor reception spaces – modelled on that of the Palazzo Ducale – containing the cycle of Tintoretto paintings that caused Ruskin to swoon in admiration.

LOCATION Campo San Rocco

VAPORETTO San Tomà

ACCESS open Monday to Friday, 10.00–13.00; Saturday and Sunday, 10.00–16.00

Bartolomeo Bon/Sante Lombardo/Scarpagnino 1515–60

RIALTO MARKET BUILDINGS
FABBRICHE VECCHIE, FABBRICHE NUOVE, PALAZZO DEI CAMERLENGHI

The blaze that reduced to rubble the whole Rialto area (except San Giacometto and the Palazzo dei Camerlenghi) on 10 January 1514 gave immediate impetus to a new, improved plan for the already well-established trading heart of Venice. The rents paid by the traders provided crucial income for the State, so the day after the fire the governing body met to discuss a quick-fix strategy. Of the seven plans put forward, it was Scarpagnino's that won the day, probably because it used the existing street plan and a simple, classical design that was both dignified and utilitarian. The first building constructed was the Fabbriche Vecchie (1520–22), on the west side of the Ruga dei Orefici and with a façade on to the Grand Canal. This stripped-back building provided offices for the judiciary on the upper levels and accommodation for different trading activities in its ground-level arcading. Scarpagnino also altered the Palazzo dei Camerlenghi (1525–28), at the foot of the Rialto bridge, which became the headquarters of the treasury magistrates and a debtors' prison.

Sansovino's Fabbriche Nuove was built 40 years after the fire (1555–56), and after Scarpagnino's death. Bordering the Grand Canal, it is similar to Scarpagnino's in its unrelenting classical form, this time on a long, narrow plot, although here there are concessions to decoration – the pediments over the windows on the upper storeys, and the more liberal use of Istrian stone. The difference between the two buildings is best seen where they abut each other overlooking the vegetable market.

LOCATION Grand Canal/Rialto market
VAPORETTO Rialto/San Silvestro
ACCESS not open to the public
VIEWPOINT Campiello Remer at Ca' Lion Morosini on the opposite bank of the Grand Canal

Antonio Abbondi (Scarpagnino)/Jacopo Sansovino 1520–56

PONTE DI RIALTO

As delicate as wedding confectionary from afar, surprisingly chunky at close quarters, and providing a broad shelter for rain-soaked gondoliers and their passengers, the Ponte di Rialto is the quintessential Venetian landmark.

The current bridge is the sixth on this site (the first, of boats, dated from around 1175) and was the only crossing of the Grand Canal until the first Ponte dell' Accademia of 1854. It is the result of a fierce 16th-century debate over the design for the replacement of the wooden drawbridge seen in Carpaccio's *Mystery of the Holy Cross at Rialto Bridge* (1494), in the Accademia. Designs by Sansovino, Vignola, Michelangelo, Scamozzi and Palladio were all rejected in favour of Da Ponte's, which, with its double row of shops linked at the top by two arches with rusticated Doric pillars and pediments, is similar in shape to its predecessor, necessitated little disruption to the neighbourhood and, crucially, achieved rent from the shopkeepers. Technologically daring, it has only a single span – at median tide level about 28 metres wide, 7.5 metres high. It is supported on 12,000 piles of elm, 6000 on each bank, each 3 metres long.

Unlike Florence's Ponte Vecchio, you can cross the Ponte Rialto on either side of the shopping arcade, thereby avoiding the crowds and enjoying uninterrupted views of the Grand Canal. From the market side, the bridge feels like a continuation of the street, the arches of the market merging with those of the bridge. On the west side are stone reliefs of Venice's patron saints, St Mark and St Theodore.

LOCATION Grand Canal/follow the signs from Piazza San Marco via Salizzada Pio X
VAPORETTO Rialto
ACCESS always open

Antonio da Ponte 1588–91

PALAZZO PISANI-MORETTA

Try to get inside this palazzo – and see probably the most complete 18th-century Venetian interior accessible to the public.

Built around 1460, the façade is the epitome of late-Venetian Gothic – a rigorously symmetrical composition enclosing superimposed multi-light window panels with quatre-foil tracery which, at second-floor level, are further refined by the introduction of semi-circular tracery. Clearly developed from the detailing at the Ca' d'Oro, the most powerful reference is, however, to the seat of the Republic's power – the Palazzo Ducale. Thus can be seen a very public connection between the individual monied families, the government of the city and the image that Venice projected to the world at the height of its power.

The Pisani-Moretta family – a branch of the Pisani – acquired it in the early 17th century. They had amassed a fortune through trade, initially dealing in Siberian fur. Their last surviving heir, Chiara, married back into the Pisani family. Widowed in 1738, between 1739 and 1746 she was to transform the building. She added a third storey and terrace and re-placed the external Gothic staircase with a striking three-branch internal stair by Andrea Tirali. The interior was similarly modernised to contemporary baroque taste. Elaborate traceried stucco work to walls and ceilings, frescoes by Tiepolo and others, and sumptuous marble and terrazzo floors ensured a formidable grandeur for the *piano nobile*. This theme, on a more domestic scale, continues in the second-floor living quarters.

LOCATION Grand Canal/land access Ramo Pisani, off Rio Terrà Dei Nomboli
VAPORETTO San Tomà
ACCESS view interior by appointment; telephone 041 5205226, fax 041 5205228
VIEWPOINT Ramo di Teatro at Sant' Angelo *vaporetto* stop

Andrea Tirali (interior stair) 15th century/18th century interior

PESCHERIA DI RIALTO
FISH MARKET

There has been a fish market in this area since the 14th century, but the present structure bordering the Grand Canal, a neo-Gothic building and part of the enthusiastic response to Ruskin's *The Stones of Venice* (1851–53), dates from 1907. It replaces a 19th-century metal and glass market building that was attached to Sansovino's Fabbriche Nuove. Designed by the engineer Annibale Forcellini, this earlier building had been heavily criticised and was demolished only ten years after its construction.

The newer building was the brainchild of Cesare Laurenti, an artist, and the architect Domenico Rupolo, and is allegedly based on buildings found in Carpaccio's paintings. Certainly it has a mock-Carpaccio chimney. It is widely regarded not only as a bad example of Venetian Gothic, with an unsatisfactory relationship between the ground-floor open loggia and the first floor, and some exaggerated Gothic features felt to lack refinement, but also as an inadequate market building. The roof is too high to provide shelter and now the fishmongers occupy the structure behind, leaving the porticoed building solely for the unloading of fish. In fact, *pace* all purists, the building is a solid and rather jolly addition to this part of the Canal, and the 'unrefined' details, such as the capitals decorated with fish and the eel- or fish-shaped gargoyle overflow pipes are amusing. Strong Moorish overtones are present in the overhung wooden roof beams and spreading capitals resting on top of the stone pillars. This is good place to begin a walk around the market area.

LOCATION Grand Canal. The Traghetto Santa Sofia crosses the Canal to the Pescheria
VAPORETTO Rialto
ACCESS ground floor always open
VIEWPOINT Traghetto Santa Sofia (Cannaregio)

Cesare Laurenti and Domenico Rupolo 1907

SANTA CROCE

SAN GIACOMO DELL'ORIO

Attached to unprepossessing houses in a quiet *campo*, San Giacomo dell'Orio has a modest air, with friendly rounded apses like those of the larger-scale Santa Maria Formosa. It must once have struck a colourful note with yellow and terracotta rendering, now faded. Founded in the 10th century, the present building dates from 1225 when it was rebuilt by the aristocratic Badoer family. The important-looking belltower with four-light mullion windows, dates from that period. Subsequent alterations from the 14th to 16th centuries have changed its appearance.

The interior is a basilica with three naves. A wide transept, also with three naves, was added in the 14th century. To make this transept, some of the chunky columns have been damaged: the left transept looks likely to collapse at any minute. Also striking is the stuccoed semicircular vault of the choir, contrasting oddly with the wooden roof. The mysterious green column in the right transept is of *verde antico* and originally from Byzantium. The medieval atmosphere of the church is largely accounted for by the splendid 14th-century ship's-keel roof, a Venetian speciality.

The Old Sacristy, containing paintings by Palma the Younger (1581), is devoted to the Eucharist, as is the chapel next to the main altar. Such chapels were popular in Venice at the end of the 16th century – a response to the Council of Trent's determination to put the Sacrament above the worship of saints and relics. Notice the 13th-century Madonna Orante, a graceful stone figure on the west wall of the right transept.

SANTA CROCE

LOCATION Campo San Giacomo dell'Orio
VAPORETTO San Stae
ACCESS open daily, 10.00–18.00; holidays, 15.00–18.00

rebuilt 1225

CAMPO SANTA MARIA MATER DOMINI

A perfect small Venetian square surrounded by predominantly early-Gothic houses, the Campo Santa Maria Mater Domini encapsulates the essence of Venetian streetscape that has hardly changed since the 13th century. Its small scale unconsciously balances the needs of thoroughfare and café seating, accommodating ground-floor shops with housing over. Central on one long side, under a projecting roof, is the 13th-century Casa degli Zane, incorporating, at first-floor level, a fine panel of four stilted-arched windows typical of the transitional style between Byzantine and Gothic – the rounded inner arch framed in a double ogee point. Above, a number of stone roundel inserts and crosses depicting animals, are let into the brickwork.

At one end of the square, the Palazzetto Viaro-Zane retains a very fine 14th-century, five-light pure Gothic window at first floor, noted by Ruskin as one of the 'earliest and loveliest of its kind in Venice'. Under the central window can be seen the remains of a lion of Venice. It is said that its addition to the building is evidence that the Republic had confiscated the property from its owners for their part in the unsuccessful 1310 attempt to overthrow the doge. The lion's subsequent defacing was part of the Napoleonic suppression of this symbol of Venice. The building's second- and third-floor façades are Renaissance additions. In the square's centre is a 14th- century wellhead. The one traditional component absent from the square itself is the church, offset in the Calle della Chiesa.

SANTA CROCE

LOCATION Campo Santa Maria Mater Domini
VAPORETTO San Stae

13th century onwards

FONDACO DEI TURCHI

Few buildings on the Grand Canal have incited such fierce debate as the Fondaco dei Turchi. On the one hand, in its detail and its massing, it represents the most powerful example of Veneto-Byzantine palace architecture. On the other, its virtual rebuilding in 1869 met with so little contemporary approval that, for some, it is now considered a 19th-century structure. Originally built by the Pesaro merchant family (see the Ca' Pesaro), its façade is one of the first to rise directly from the waterfront – the traditional two-storey accommodation of ground-level warehousing and first-floor living apartments planned around a central court. It has a remarkably open and broad frontage of stilted Byzantine arcading enclosed between two towers – architectural vestiges of a more defensive Eastern style. This horizontality contrasts with the later narrower and more intensively developed Grand Canal structures.

In 1381 the building was acquired by the Republic – initially to be gifted to the Este family as reward for their support in the Chioggian war and later to accommodate all manner of important city visitors. Its current name relates to its function from 1621 to 1838 as the trading post for Eastern merchants. During this period it was internally transformed to work as a largely self-contained Muslim community – incorporating mosque and bathhouse. Abandoned in 1838, it fell into the dereliction that caused Ruskin to label it a 'ghastly ruin' and initiate the campaign for its restoration.

LOCATION Grand Canal/Fondaco dei Turchi
VAPORETTO San Stae
ACCESS currently closed for restoration (site of the Natural History Museum)
VIEWPOINT Campo San Marcuola (Cannaregio)

early 13th century/rebuilt 1869 Federico Berchet

DEPOSITO DEL MEGIO
GRAIN STORE

Standing on the Grand Canal, between the startlingly restored 13th-century Veneto-Byzantine Fondaco dei Turchi and Longhena's 17th-century Palazzo Belloni-Battagia, is an austere brick and stone-detailed façade with a crenellated roofline – the Deposito del Megio. Although easily missed among the surrounding grandeur, this is a vital building dating from the height of Venice's power – one of a series of granaries erected to store the grain produced on its mainland territories. The Republic's largest grain stores – controversially demolished by Napoleon in order to create the Royal Gardens – were at San Marco. Together with the flour warehouse at San Silvestro, these supplied the day-to-day needs of the Venetian people. However, the location of the Deposito del Megio – away from the busiest areas of the city, primarily geared to access from the water – and its 'fortress' quality of design has led some commentators to speculate that its primary purpose was protection against the consequences of famine in time of harvest failure or the shortages that would result from prolonged siege. The 15th-century façade is original, with the exception of the lion of St Mark – a 20th-century replacement for the one removed by Napoleon. In overall appearance the façade is reminiscent of trading posts, *fondaci*, such as would have been seen, for example, in the eastern port of Alexandria, and represents a Venetian interpretation of an oriental building type. Today the building has been incorporated into a primary-school complex.

LOCATION Grand Canal/Calle del Megio
VAPORETTO San Stae
ACCESS not open to the public
VIEWPOINT San Marcuola landing stage

15th century

CA' PESARO

In the mid 16th century the Pesaro family began buying up parcels of land to create the site of this imposing baroque palace – Baldassare Longhena's last major work and one of the grandest pieces of 17th-century Venetian secular architecture. Stylistically it rejects the Venetian tradition and follows the Roman precedent first seen in Sansovino's Palazzo Corner della Ca' Grande. The concern to ally Venice with antiquity and legitimise its empire building by reference to Roman history was again to the fore.

Ca' Pesaro's monumental structure dominates the Grand Canal, and because, unusually, the side façade is visible, it appears extraordinarily solid. The site is particularly deep. Twin portals, set within the diamond-pointed rusticated ground storey, open from the Grand Canal on to a massive *pòrtego* which runs back into a rear courtyard of tiered *loggie*. Twinned columns to the main façade emphasise the grand central hall at upper levels and the whole becomes a theatrical, three-dimensional, multi-layered composition. Giovanni Pesaro died in 1658 (his extraordinary funerary monument by Longhena is in the Frari), and work continued for the next 20 years under his nephew Leonardo who, by 1682, had completed the first-floor façade. But in this year both architect and patron died and building work ceased for many years. It was finally completed in 1710 by Longhena's follower, Antonio Gaspari.

LOCATION Grand Canal/Fondamenta Pesaro
VAPORETTO San Stae
ACCESS open Tuesday to Sunday, 10.00–17.00
(now the Museum of Modern Art/Oriental Museum)
VIEWPOINT Calle del Traghetto, off Campo San
Felice (Cannaregio)

Baldassare Longhena, Antonio Gaspari c 1650–1710

SAN STAE

San Stae (Venetian for St Eustace) was founded in the 10th century, but was rebuilt extensively, probably in the 16th century and then again in 1678 by Giovanni Grassi, who reoriented it to face the Grand Canal. Over a hundred years passed, however, before a competition was instigated for the façade. Twelve designs, including one by Andrea Tirali, an early exponent of neoclassicism, were put forward, but Rossi, nephew of Giuseppe Sardi and greatly influenced by him as well as by Longhena, won the day with this exuberant façade, enlivened by sculptures by Giuseppe Torretto and Antonio Corradini. Doge Alvise II Mocenigo, who lived in the parish, financed the project.

Although the façade has baroque elements, for instance the scroll under the central broken pediment that supports sculpted figures, it also has neo-Palladian/neoclassical elements – note the half Corinthian columns standing on high bases, and the triangular pediment. The façade was a watershed in that it marked the end of a 200-year tradition whereby a façade had commemorated its patron in increasingly grandiose fashion (see, for example, Santa Maria del Giglio). This façade marked a return to the Venetian tradition of *mediocritas* (see Introduction, page 0.13), and was probably ordered by the doge himself, who opted to be buried here with little ceremony. The interior is white marble and *marmorino* – recently cleaned and almost blinding.

Just to the left of the church is an early-18th-century building, once the Scoletta dei Battioro (goldsmiths) by Giovan Giacomo Gaspari, a loser in the façade competition.

LOCATION Grand Canal/Campo San Stae, best reached by *vaporetto*
VAPORETTO San Stae
ACCESS open 10.00–18.00; Sunday and holidays, 15.00–18.00

Giovanni Grassi/façade by Domenico Rossi 1678/1790

PALAZZO MOCENIGO AT SAN STAE

The Mocenigo was one of the great Venetian families, first settling in Venice around the year 1000. Between the early 15th and 18th centuries seven doges were elected from its ranks. As befitting such stature, the family first lived on the Grand Canal, in San Marco, where the façades of its four adjoining palazzi (opposite today's San Tomà *vaporetto* stop) reflect its increasing power and fortune. However, in the mid 16th century the family split – the second branch moving into Santa Croce and creating the Palazzo Mocenigo at San Stae.

The inclusion of this building in our guide is entirely due to its magnificently preserved 18th/19th century interior – one of very few open to the public. It not only captures the opulence of the closing years of the Venetian Republic, but also reminds the visitor that not all wealth fled the city at the time of the Republic's fall. This branch of the Mocenigo continued to live here until 1954 when the last family member donated the palazzo to the city.

Its layout reflects the needs of a typical wealthy merchant family. At ground level are the storage rooms which open off the *pòrtego*, a central large entrance hall that spans between the water frontage and the land access. The grand staircase rises to the first and second floors to similarly vast central reception rooms leading through to living accommodation. The scale and opulence leave the visitor in no doubt as to the importance of the family. The frescoed decoration commemorates the achievements of the Mocenigo.

LOCATION Salizzada San Stae
VAPORETTO San Stae
ACCESS open Tuesday to Sunday, 10.00–16.00

18th/19th century interior

TOBACCO FACTORY

Nestling behind the Piazzale Roma in a surprisingly quiet backwater is this old factory – a collection of buildings lining the Rio delle Burchielle, rendered in a warm terracotta colour. The oldest part of the building is the section around the front doorway, with the lozenge-shaped windows on either side, an interrupted cornice and triangular pediment with clock above. During Venice's attempt in the 19th and early 20th centuries to industrialise – see, for example, Molino Stucky and Dreher Brewery on Giudecca – the building was gradually extended – especially in 1840–50 by Giuseppe Mezzani. The distinctive, medieval-style covered bridge linking the buildings on either side of the *rio* dates from the 1920s. It has two walkways, one above the other, and an attractive arch decorated with Istrian stone.

On the far side of the bridge are unrenovated parts of the factory, with giant dormer windows on the top storey. The big arched windows with metal grills and fan-shaped, segmented glass along with the heavy, battered Istrian stone base and rendered brick façade give a pleasingly solid look to this industrial complex.

LOCATION Rio delle Burchielle, just off Piazzale Roma
VAPORETTO Piazzale Roma
ACCESS not open to the public

Giuseppe Mezzani (19th-century buildings) 1786–1928

INA GARAGE

7.18

Compared with the splendour of Piazza San Marco, this ocean liner of a rationalist building may lack charm, but it is worth considering that, just as the Palazzo Ducale represented the wealth and might of the Serenissima, the INA garage was much vaunted by the press of the day as a symbol of Venetian superiority. When completed, it was the largest multi-storey car park in the world and the modern gateway to the city, providing fitting accommodation for cars arriving over the newly constructed Ponte della Libertà (1933).

There were, of course, contrary views. The motor link to the mainland was highly contentious – doom-mongers were convinced that Venice's buildings would soon be 'ringing to the roar of motor cars and swathed in billowing fumes'. The garage too was controversial. Certain restrictions had been placed on the building with the aim of concealing motorised traffic, but because so many buildings were demolished in the immediate surroundings the garage nevertheless stands out starkly in the Piazzale Roma.

Better close up than from a distance, the façade is clean with crisp detailing, the ribbon-like windows turning seamlessly around the corners of the building like the lanes of a motorway. The hemispherical projections at each end hide two internal cylindrical ramps, one to take cars up, the other to take them down. These ramps are lit by windows at the top under flat roofs with concrete 'wheel-spoke' supports. The interior is well maintained and boldly painted, the entrance/exit railings made of wrought iron with jolly glass panels in a blue and gold swirl design.

SANTA CROCE

LOCATION Piazzale Roma
VAPORETTO Piazzale Roma
ACCESS always open

Eugenio Miozzi 1931–34

INAIL HEADQUARTERS

This development of insurance offices and apartments, standing in the *calle* to the left of San Simeon across the Grand Canal from the railway station, is viewed by many Italian commentators as a landmark in post-war Venetian architecture. At first sight, however, it may look like a confusion of architectural elements with little relation either to its immediate context or to the greater historical Venetian tradition. It is not helped by its current state of repair nor the negative associations that many observers may now have to its 'modernist' style – a style that is inherently international and often denies site-specific traditions. In its façade can be read the architects' struggle to find an appropriate contemporary architectural expression for Venice without resorting to pastiche.

The building is concrete-framed, with a predominately horizontal emphasis, further broken down into a series of cells, framed by tapering pilasters and incorporating asymmetrical stone and brick detailing. Liberated from the structural restrictions of load-bearing walls, Samonà described the design as 'a series of continuously vibrating icons which repudiates the basic difference between solid and void... an architectural continuity which avoids allusions to the iconographical traditions of the city, while retaining the city's relatively small proportions in its single parts'.

LOCATION Calle Nuova di San Simeone
VAPORETTO Stazione
ACCESS not open to the public

Giuseppe Samonà and Egle Trincanato 1952–56

SCHOOL OF ARCHITECTURE ENTRANCE

In the 1960s the University of Venice School of Architecture moved to the site of the Tolentini monastery. Scarpa, then Dean of the University, was asked to design an entrance through the Campazzo dei Tolentini, wedged between San Nicolò dei Tolentini, the monastery itself (both 17th–18th centuries) and a small house. During restoration, the builders discovered a Renaissance marble doorway. Instead of reinstating the door as a conventional entrance, Scarpa made it a focal point of the Campazzo by leaving it on the ground and turning it into a pool. Scarpa died in 1978 and his assistant, Sergio Los, worked from Scarpa's plans. The pool's water reflects the diverse architecture of the Campazzo, where the side façade of the Tolentini towers over it, providing a synthesis of old and new. It also enlarges the perceived space in the courtyard, gives life to the activities of passers-by and echoes the waterscape beyond. Unfortunately, the pool is often empty! The pediment of the doorway points towards a gate of sliding iron railings, protected by a slab of Istrian stone supported by two inclined walls that reflect sunlight into the otherwise shady space. The striation of the stonework on the gateway echoes the shapes of the pool.

You can walk through the gate to the old cloisters and sometimes get into the library and refectory. The church itself was designed by Scamozzi. The awe-inspiring façade with its Corinthian portico and neoclassical pediment by Andrea Tirali is the best bit.

LOCATION Campazzo dei Tolentini, near the Giardino Papadopoli
VAPORETTO Piazzale Roma
ACCESS church open daily, 8.00-12.00 and 16.30-19.00. In term time you can walk through the university entrance to admire Scarpa's entrance and the cloisters beyond

Carlo Scarpa/Sergio Los 1978

GIUDECCA

REDENTORE

If temples are to be built outside the city, then their façades will be made in such a way as to look over the public streets and over the rivers, so that those passing by can see them and make their salutations ... Palladio

Along with San Giorgio Maggiore and the Zitelle, the Redentore completes the tripartite Palladian Lagoon panorama. All are best viewed from a distance, the Redentore from the Fondamenta delle Zattere. From here it is possible to see Palladio's intention: to build a perfectly proportioned classical temple, more restrained than San Giorgio, where each exterior element works in harmony. Completed by da Ponte after Palladio's death in 1580, the Redentore (redeemer) is a votive church, commissioned by the Senate after the 1575–76 plague. On the feast of the Redeemer (third Sunday in July) the doge crossed to the Redentore on a bridge of boats, an event now marked by a spectacular festival.

The interior, newly cleaned, is more intimate and assured than that of San Giorgio Maggiore, the white stone in stark contrast with the black baroque altar statuary by Girolamo Campagna. The longitudinal plan conformed to the liturgical needs of the Capuchins. It is in three parts: the wide nave, bordered with interconnecting chapels, leads to a central 'trefoil' space – accommodating important visitors – lit by windows under the dome. The heavy cornice around the nave leads the eye to the unique semicircle of columns that stands guard behind the altar and hides the monks' choir beyond.

LOCATION Fondamenta San Giacomo, Giudecca
VAPORETTO Redentore
ACCESS open weekdays, 10.00–17.00; Sundays, 13.00–17.00

Palladio/Antonio da Ponte 1577–92

MOLINO STUCKY

The massive Molino Stucky – built as a pasta mill and for grain storage – is a powerful reminder of Venice's unsuccessful early-20th-century attempts to industrialise, particularly on the Giudecca. (After the First World War, most such development was to transfer to the mainland Porto Marghera near Mestre.) Not only its scale and use, but also its style – an overbearing northern European Gothic – were alien to the islands. It is said that Giovanni Stucky – one of Venice's wealthiest citizens at the time and owner of the Palazzo Grassi – gained permission to convert and expand the original mill structure by threatening that he would otherwise close his business and make the workforce redundant. Probably as ruthless an employer as negotiator, in 1910 Stucky was shot dead at the railway station by one of his employees. Despite this inauspicious history, however, the nine storeys of meticulously detailed Gothic brickwork – their immense blind arcading, whimsical turrets and crenellated battlements – are impressive. The architectural theme can also be seen in the nearby Dreher Brewery.

Giudecca's failure to work as an industrial centre compounded the business' decline and the factory finally closed in 1954. After almost half a century's neglect, this vast complex is finally being converted into a series of apartments overlooking the Giudecca Canal. They are programmed for completion in 2002, while a luxury hotel, incorporating the spired corner tower, and international conference centre are scheduled for 2005.

LOCATION Fondamenta San Biagio
VAPORETTO Sant' Eufemia
ACCESS currently not open to the public

E Wullekopf, G Boccanegra (restoration) 1897–1920; restoration and conversion 1999–

HOUSING AT DREHER BREWERY

Most contemporary public housing in Venice – which presents a challenge for architects up against traditional thinkers within the Commune – is found on the margins of the main island. Currently, it is the Giudecca which is attracting the most creative activity.

Built in the shadow of the Molino Stucky complex, this former brewery adopted a similar German Gothic style to create a massive brick industrial building. After falling into disuse, in the 1980s the building was converted to provide the housing seen today – outside the street pattern and with limited public access. To effect its conversion the architect has opened up the core of the building to create a central atrium – three large glazed roof lanterns inserted into the existing roof can be seen from across the Giudecca canal. All upper-level housing units are reached from the atrium, via internal access galleries. At ground-floor level, around the perimeter, there is a series of small housing units with direct external stair access. The light and insubstantial visible design additions – in the form of steps, balustrading, access landings and bridges in metal and glass – contrast with the monumental form and detailing of the original brick structure. This is particularly striking to the rear of the building where escape-route bridges provide a link with the former industrial chimney.

GIUDECCA

LOCATION Fondamenta San Biagio
VAPORETTO Giudecca/Sant' Eufemia
ACCESS interior not open to the public

C Fano and U Vigevano 1909–20/G Gambirasio restoration and conversion 1985–90

CASA DE MARIA

If you are in doubt as to what style your house should be, opt for something familiar. When designing his studio overlooking the Bacino di San Marco, the artist Mario de Maria went for the most familiar of all building styles, Venetian Gothic, with obvious references to the decorative elements of the Palazzo Ducale. Such imitation is a time-honoured tradition, prefigured, for example, by the Ca' d'Oro, but whereas the latter is considered a reverential bow to the Palazzo Ducale, which also brought kudos to the family concerned, de Maria's house is usually described as an ironic and highly ostentatious caricature.

The most obvious references to the Palazzo Ducale are the stonework frieze topping the façade, the quatrefoil design embedded in the decorative top central window, and the pattern of the brickwork – not seen on any other domestic building in Venice. But this unique private house is more than a reference to Venice's glorious history. With its large windows, designed to bring light to the studio within, the semi-circular wrought-iron balconies with fluted stone supports – the support to the central window is connected delicately to the main portal – this florid little building seeks to develop Gothic in both a personal and a practical way.

At first sight, the Casa de Maria is a somewhat inappropriate neighbour to the Zitelle, but the shape of the windows of the *piano nobile* do echo, perhaps intentionally, the tripartite window on the upper storey of Palladio's church.

LOCATION Giudecca, next to the Zitelle church
VAPORETTO Zitelle
ACCESS not open to the public

Mario de Maria 1910–13

VILLA HÉRIOTT

Facing south with uninterrupted views over the open Lagoon, albeit today incongruous in an area of modern housing, this luxurious, peaceful villa – now restored – houses a children's home and the International University of Art. The villa was built by a Frenchman, Conte Hériott, who pitched up on a yacht and decided to stay. His widow left the villa to the Commune on the condition that it was used as a school. Walk through the gate with its neo-Gothic, terracotta roof and stroll around the garden.

The H-shaped neo-Byzantine/Gothic building has eclectic detailing drawn from Venetian architectural history. The brick façade of the main building has Istrian stone window surrounds, quoins and fretted eaves protecting a geometric art-nouveau-style tiled frieze. The windows, some balustraded in various stone patterns, others forming a corbelled bay with overhanging roof, are Veneto-Byzantine with Gothic and classical features. The Istrian stone columns supporting the porch all have different capitals, some with heads, and the marble panels with dentillated surrounds below the windows on the lower level are all imaginatively carved. Inside the main building, the double-height vestibule is like a medieval hunting lodge, with stone staircases (one going nowhere), soaring up to the second storey, and brick walls dotted with stone reliefs, trophies and plaques.

In the grounds are a boathouse with spreading wooden capitals and overhanging roof (being restored, 2001), and a large summerhouse used as a library, completely surrounded by a covered terrace.

LOCATION Calle Michelangelo
VAPORETTO Zitelle
ACCESS grounds open during term time. Ask permission to look around inside

Paolo Mainella 1929

IACP COMPLEX

Another interesting contemporary housing development is the IACP at the west end of Giudecca. There are many echoes of traditional Venetian architectural elements on display here – the immediate relationship with water, the narrow alleys or *calli* and an emphasis on the vertical. Its main public façades front on to water – the Canale dei Lavraneri and the Rio di San Biagio – with paired blocks of crisply detailed brick and concrete housing units rising sheer from the waterfront. These are separated by a narrow *calle* running back from the water's edge, where owners' boats are moored, into the centre. Within the complex, a series of stepped terraces rises to four storeys on a forest of tightly spaced brick *piloti* supporting high-level access decks. At roof level, arched planes of concrete with oculi shield terraces.

The whole is laid out on a rigorous grid aligned with the brick chimney of the adjacent Molino Stucky building. The detailing is severe and precise but despite the tight spaces the scale and lightness of the structure allows natural light to flood into the ground level and, generally, avoid gloom. There is no doubt, however, that the physical density borders on the claustrophobic and that this, coupled with the absence of apparent occupation, creates a feeling of unease. In so doing, on the other hand, it perhaps captures a traditional attribute of Venetian public space.

LOCATION Calle Larga dei Lavraneri/Campiello Priuli
VAPORETTO Sant'Eufemia/Sacca Fisola
ACCESS not open to the public

Gino Valle and assistants 1980–86

EX-ICE FACTORY HOUSING

A number of housing developments cluster around the Zitelle vaporetto landing stage in the Campo di Marte quarter – a run-down area of former working-class accommodation. Pastor's housing development is revealed behind the modest white-rendered façade of this former ice factory. Working within the shell of the building, the whole has been opened up to form an internal access court reminiscent of a church nave – a series of curved apsidal volumes punctuating a strong rhythm of brickwork columns and first-floor connecting bridges. This calm private oasis behind a frequently bustling water frontage leads to three storeys of residential accommodation. The outward façades face the adjoining Calle Michelangelo and seen from the rear show considerable skill and sensitivity in fashioning a new use for a very particular industrial building. The new work stitched into the existing structure has been meticulously considered and detailed to create a rich layering of historic references – from the sweeping copper guttering to the round oculi windows and ground-level arching brickwork.

An interesting, contrasting reuse of industrial premises can be seen in the adjacent massive red-rendered blocks by Nani Valle and Giorgio Bellavitis. Here, internal courts have been carved out to extend the public routes away from the water frontage. Five storeys of apartments enclose the courts, adopting elements from traditional Venetian domestic architecture. Compare their scale and detailing with the Zattere flats facing them across the Giudecca canal.

LOCATION Fondamenta delle Zitelle
VAPORETTO Zitelle
ACCESS not open to the public

Valeriano Pastor with Michelina Michelotto and Barbara Pastor, EDIL Venezia 1993–95

ZAGGIA, EX-BAKERY HOUSING

Located behind the ice factory, this development further enriches the street pattern and reinforces the architectural continuity of the area in line with the overall 1989 masterplan for the Campo di Marte quarter. Viewed from the Calle Michelangelo, the two- storey structure incorporates the former bakery and maintains a variety of shop units with refurbished housing units above. Stand back from this and the new housing behind is revealed, reaching over the existing buildings and accessed from a parallel new *calle*. Although rising to four storeys, the scale of the development has been sensitively handled and grows organically from the existing structures. It is meticulously detailed in brick and concrete. Deep reveals to the windows house shutters, and steeply raking terrazzo cills reinforce a feeling of permanence. Particular attention has been given to the transition from public to semi-public and private space, confidently handled through careful use of materials – brick, concrete and metal – and the creation of landscaped areas within a pattern of access stairs, ramps and lift to the units. Existing refurbished façades interlock with the new, with numerous references to traditional Venetian architecture.

The intent to recreate street patterns and reinstate life in neglected areas is common to many new housing developments – other examples include the Mazzorbo and San Giobbe housing. However, the success in this quarter is self-evident and should be reinforced by the nearby Aldo Rossi development currently under construction.

GIUDECCA

LOCATION Calle Michelangelo
VAPORETTO Zitelle
ACCESS not open to the public

Luca Rossi, EDIL Venezia 1994–99

HOUSING AT FORMER JUNGHANS FACTORY

Conversion of the former Junghans armaments factory complex is one of the most ambitious urban projects currently underway. It is located on the southern edge of the island, and can be approached from the Corte Grande, where a rare example of 1930s modern movement industrial architecture is currently being converted into apartments with a supermarket at ground level. From here a bridge link connects to the main complex – an island within an island. At its heart is the so-called 'bunker', a triangular bastion, formerly the site of the explosives storage, which has been reclad and re-worked to provide upper level one- and two- bedroom apartments, over lower storeys containing recreational and conference facilities. To the north, set against its original industrial chimney, is a new waterside apartment block – a flush cube in grey render with white stone surrounds defining the windows and doors. Its volume replaces a former industrial building, one storey lower. With the windows set flush, balcony doors set back and reveals coloured in dark grey, the façade becomes a play of geometry against a crisp cubic form. Nearby there is a series of conversions to provide a mix of housing for sale and rent plus student accommodation, with infills to complete the pattern of traditional streets and squares and, at the same time retain the softer, greener more domestic scale that differentiates Giudecca from the intense urban development of the central islands.

LOCATION Corte Grande/Fondamenta delle Scuole
VAPORETTO Palanca
ACCESS no internal access

Cino Zucchi and associates 1998–

LIDO

HOTEL EXCELSIOR

This sprawling battleship of a building was conceived by Nicolò Spada, later to found the CIGA chain of hotels, as a palatial seafront home for entertainment on the grand scale. Although the Lido had occupied a strategic position in Venice's seafaring history, its barrenness and soft sands had always militated against large-scale development. However, lengthy negotiations, in the face of incredulous objections by the authorities, eventually resulted in permission to build. First, however, the ground level had to be consolidated and raised by more than 2 metres to create a practical base for construction. Giovanni Sardi then went to work, unfettered by the design restrictions that faced architects working in the Venetian centre, to create a bizarre mixture of Moorish domes and minarets, Veneto-Byzantine features, bowdlerised art nouveau and louche Edwardian splendour.

The first part to be built, originally Spada's palace (now part of the hotel's east wing), was completed in 1907, after just 17 months. It was inaugurated with a banquet and firework display that attracted huge attention in Venice and boosted tourism on the Lido. In 1908 the palace became a hotel.

Architecturally at the point where Las Vegas meets the Alhambra, as a luxury hotel, the Excelsior is unique, peacefully located, and well worth a detour. Check out the Moorish court on the ground floor, the seaward and roadside façades – a fascinating mix of oriental detail and unresolved rhythm – and the Sala degli Stucchi, a third-floor banqueting room, its original decoration newly restored. (see also Spada's home at Villa Monplaisir.)

LOCATION Lungomare Marconi, Lido. Take a bus or walk from the *vaporetto*
VAPORETTO Lido–Santa Maria Elisabetta
ACCESS all year round

Giovanni Sardi 1898–1908

VILLA MONPLAISIR

One of the earliest villas to be built on the Lido – as a wealthy citizen's escape from the physical and stylistic claustrophobia of Venice's historic centre – Monplaisir is perhaps the seminal example of the Venetian art nouveau. It was built for the hotelier Nicolò Spada (see Hotel Excelsior). The building seen today has been much altered over the years, its outlook blocked in by shop units, and the whole kept in a poor state of repair. Nevertheless, its inventive design and its quality of craftsmanship shine through in the surviving glazed tilework, decorative metalwork – balustrading and gutter brackets – and idiosyncratic stonework carving. Contemporary photographs show that, in contrast with today's grey render, the façades were originally intensively decorated in flowing art nouveau designs. In this it was a domestic precursor of Sullam's later more formal use of the same device in his Commercial Building on Bacino Orseolo in San Marco. Originally crowning the whole, but now also lost, was a fantastical *altana* – the traditional Venetian roof terrace raised over the pitched roof – of serpentine metalwork.

While the stylistic references to mainland European architecture of the time are clear – such as the work of Hector Guimard in Paris and Otto Wagner in Vienna – Sullam has taken the spirit of art nouveau and created a recognisably Venetian piece of architecture.

LOCATION Santa Maria Elisabetta (Gran Viale), at junction with Via Lepanto
VAPORETTO Lido–Santa Maria Elisabetta
ACCESS not open to the public

Guido Costante Sullam 1904–05

HOTEL DES BAINS

Made famous by Visconti's film *Death in Venice* (1971) as the place where Dirk Bogarde's character Aschenbach falls for Tadzio, the young boy who is to be his undoing, the Hotel des Bains, despite the solid mass of its neo-classical façade, still has an attractive period charm. Perfectly situated along the main beach, it is a monument to the huge drive in the early years of the 20th century to make the Lido a tourist destination. This ambition also resulted in the instigation of the Biennale and its pavilions, the Hotel Excelsior and the opulent villas that line the streets behind the Lido front. The style of the Hotel des Bains, cool and elegant, could not be more different from the earlier and far more ebulliant Excelsior further down the Lungomare.

Much of the charm of the place, once you've experienced the private beach over the road, is to be found inside. The Sala Visconti, for example, is fully wood-panelled in Liberty style, complete with ornate balconies and mirrors. The breakfast room, with French windows and arched sectioned windows on two sides of the room, still has the original wooden floor and a cross-beamed, sectioned and gold-decorated ceiling . A smaller dining room, leading off this room, is similar in style. For the well-heeled this is indeed a delightful retreat.

LOCATION Lungomare Marconi, Lido. Walk or take a bus from the *vaporetto* stop
VAPORETTO Lido–Santa Maria Elisabetta
ACCESS open all year

Francesco Marsich 1905–09

HUNGARIA PALACE HOTEL

Only reopened as a hotel in May 1999 by its current owner after years of neglect and a very speedy refurbishment, the façade of this hotel is a one-off. Clad almost entirely in ceramic tiles, which include images of cherubs, semi-clad women and the ubiquitous lion of Venice, it is a slightly worn monument to turn-of-the-last-century 'Venetian secessionist' style, with Veneto-Byzantine touches in the windows.

The hotel was the brainchild of a hotelier, Ludovico Fabrizio, who oversaw the building and commissioned the famous Milanese cabinet-maker Eugenio Quarti to make furniture specifically for the Hungaria Palace rooms. Today, much of this furniture has been restored and is still *in situ*, ignored by looters who swept through when the hotel was closed, because at some point during its history it had been painted blue.

In 1914, Fabrizio asked Luigi Fabris, an artist, sculptor and ceramicist from Bassano, to clad the façade in ceramic tiles. The name Ausonia Palace Hotel was adopted in 1920, after the war against Austria and Hungary. Because a conservation order was later slapped on the building, the name on the façade has not been changed back.

Inside, much of the original decoration, executed by a Viennese company, has been removed, destroyed or covered up in the refurbishment. Nevertheless, the bar and other public rooms still contain some of the original Liberty-style décor, and the conservatory/dining room is very attractive, with the original stained-glass windows. The current owner hopes to continue the restoration.

LOCATION Gran Viale, Lido, near the *vaporetto* stop
VAPORETTO Lido–Santa Maria Elisabetta
ACCESS open all year

Luigi Fabrizio, Luigi Fabris 1905–15

LIDO VILLAS
VIA DARDANELLI AND VIA DANDOLO

The villa-laden streets of the Lido date from the first quarter of the 20th century and were built with glorious disregard for the controls imposed on architects working in the city centre. Many streets are worth a stroll, but we concentrate on a small area to the south-west of the main shopping street – Via Dandolo and Via Dardanelli. These two streets are lined with noteworthy super-homes – in Veneto-Byzantine and Gothic-revivalist style, and in the Venetian versions of art nouveau and art deco.

Approached along the Via Dandolo, note No. 26, a Palazzo Ducale look-alike; No. 22 (at the corner of Via Lepanto), an extraordinary villa-style block of apartments with a first-floor Renaissance-style loggia painted with art-nouveau floral decorations; and No. 20, sporting the lion of St Mark, garish yellow capitals to the columns supporting the fence and a plethora of art nouveau details.

Turn into the Via Dardanelli for a further range of exceptional homes. At No. 22 is the Villino Gemma. Notable here is the façade paintwork and tile decoration: *trompe l'oeil* rustication to the ground storey, painted frieze to the upper story, and trefoil decoration on the the roof eaves. Also note the blue tiled panels over the windows and the ceramic frieze of orange and lemon trees. At first floor is a light and airy loggia, independently roofed and supported on delicate stone columns with Byzantine capitals. The wrought-iron gate in an elaborate rose design is spoilt by the surrounding pink majolica tiles, but the overall flavour of the villa, with the top-storey reference to an *altana* and an overall air of repose, is impressive. The delight of No. 42, La Barbera, painted in a typical Venetian palette of pale terracotta and yellow, is its roof-level ceramic frieze of lemon fruits, contained within the oversized eaves support brackets.

At the corner of the Via Dardanelli and Via Foscari is a complex of modern apartments (1987–90) by Alessandro Scarpa. Built ten years after his Condominio Villa

early 20th century

LIDO VILLAS

Morosini, it is a dramatically stripped-back version of that development. Simply detailed, the massing of the buildings is reminiscent of children's building block shapes: cylinders juxtaposed with triangles, squares, parallelograms and hexagons. Cladding panels vary with each block – stripes of blue and white, grey and white – but the aluminium-clad mansards, projecting upper-level windows, metal stacked balconies and *altana*-type roof terraces are common to all blocks.

For those preferring an ecclesiastical feel to their home, No. 50–52 is an early-20th-century villa with the air of a folly or cottage orné built in the shape of a church – its faux campanile rising to enclose a single room. Its façades – white rendered and punctuated with a series of paired, single and arched semicircular windows – nod to historic precedent, but are largely a creation of the architect's imagination. The gable-end façade, terminating at roof level with the brickwork arcading traditionally found on Venetian Gothic churches, completes the fantasy. The whole is entered through a Gothic-revival gateway like that found at the Villa Hériott.

LOCATION Lido, a walk from the *vaporetto* through the shopping centre
VAPORETTO Lido–Santa Maria Elisabetta
ACCESS villas are not open to the public

early 20th century

SANTA MARIA DELLA VITTORIA
TEMPIO VOTIVO

Today, the neglected appearance of this work by Giuseppe Torres belies its importance. Its design, exhibited at the first Roman Biennale in 1921, was conceived as a church dedicated to the important 10th-century icon of the Madonna of Nicopeia, brought from Constantinople and now housed in the north transept of San Marco. Torres' intent was to bind symbolically the newly developing Lido with the main island by creating a contemporary mirror of the Salute, but using a style which rejected revivalism while maintaining historical continuity. Before its construction, however, the design was further pared back to a set of visual prompts that echo Venice's classical past.

A tall flight of steps – set on an axis aligned with San Marco and flanked by towers – arrives at the elevated circular portico enclosing a high-domed central drum. Now called the Votive Temple, the building has become a mausoleum and work is currently underway to reopen the main central space as a war memorial. The building has clearly not fulfilled the architect's original ambition and has also had to contend with negative associations with the so-called Fascist style of Italian architecture. However, it is a clear example of one architect's attempt to find an appropriate contemporary Venetian architectural expression, and is in stark contrast to his previous work, such as the revivalist Casa Torres.

LOCATION Riviera Santa Maria Elisabetta
VAPORETTO Lido–Santa Maria Elisabetta
ACCESS under internal restoration in 2001

Giuseppe Torres 1920–24

HOUSE OF THE PHARMACIST

One of two houses by Brenno del Giudice on the Lido, this little villa is a pleasing mix of styles, including late Renaissance, baroque and art nouveau. Here del Giudice, sometime lecturer at the Venetian School of Architecture, has taken full advantage of the freedom given to architects working outside the city centre and provided a house quite in keeping with the decorative and personalised architecture prevalent on the Lido. His later buildings, the fire station in Dorsoduro for example, and a house constructed on the Cannaregio canal, embrace modernism, without the organic charm of this house.

The baroque shell design evident in the middle window on the first floor is taken up in the curved cornice shading the shop windows on the ground floor, (which appears to be influenced by art nouveau), the arched top floor window and the swirling buttresses supporting the window on the upper level. The first-floor balconies are similarly baroque in feel. On the other hand, the side façade, which includes traditionally Venetian lozenge-shaped windows and a reference to an *altana* at roof level, is indicative of an architect looking forward to the modernist era.

LOCATION Via Sandro Gallo (junction with Via Quattro Fontane)
VAPORETTO Lido–Santa Maria Elisabetta
ACCESS not open to the public

Brenno del Giudice 1926–27

PALAZZO DEL CASINO AND PALAZZO DEL CINEMA

If the Hotel Excelsior is a building to encourage decadence, then the rationalist 1930s' architecture of its neighbour, the Palazzo del Casino appears to be giving the opposite message. A building less likely to induce reckless gambling is hard to imagine. Stripped of references to any style, it is reminiscent of Santa Maria Vittoria but with less charm. The building is used as a casino only during the summer; those determined to lose their money in winter must indulge themselves on the main island at the Palazzo Loredan-Vendramin-Calergi.

The original Palazzo del Cinema is equally stark, but is at least relieved by a curved end wall of windows and horizontal concrete detailing. This is now virtually obliterated, however, by the 1950s' front-of-house extension. Slightly more jaunty with its zig-zag concrete canopy over the central entrance, and similarly shaped 'arches', it has the appropriate appearance of a row of beach huts. This is the venue of the annual Venice Film Festival, when the Lido buzzes with glitterati, many of whom lodge at the Hotel Excelsior over the road. Plans for a rebuild of the cinema are now in progress.

Whatever one's view of architecture dating from the Fascist era, this complex is certainly at odds with nearby buildings constructed earlier in the 20th century – not just the exuberant Hotel Excelsior but also the building on the corner of the Via Candia, currently housing the Lion Bar.

LOCATION Lungomare Marconi, Lido, near the Hotel Excelsior

VAPORETTO Lido–Santa Maria Elisabetta

ACCESS casino open April to September; cinema houses the Venice Film Festival in August/September

Casino E Miozzi 1936–38/Cinema L Quagliata 1936–37, extension A Scattolin 1952

VILLA CALABI

Although now functioning as four apartments, this building was designed as the home and office of its architect, Daniele Calabi. It is a rigorous reinterpretation of a traditional palazzetto – fusing the austerity of modern-movement architecture with many historic Venetian design elements. Rising from a stone lower-storey, two levels of accommodation are topped by a glazed and timber-clad clerestory under a widely oversailing roof. First appearances might suggest a solid brick-built structure, but closer viewing shows that the architect has made no attempt to disguise that this is in fact a concrete-framed building. Facing materials are no more than cladding creating shallow, sharply detailed façades. This is particularly evident at the second-floor corner balcony, where the terracotta 'brick' cladding is precisely cut back from the balcony and its bracketed supports to show clearly the method of construction. Above, the corner column of the concrete frame has minimal decoration which hints at the historical precedent of stone column and capital – a device repeated in the paired windows with their undercill panels on the façade facing the Via Dalmazia. Rising over the whole is a contemporary interpretation of the Venetian chimney.

This house was erected on the site of an earlier villa, and it is possible that the device of the clerestory takes the place of the decorative frieze typically found in early-20th-century villas such as, for instance, in the nearby Via Dardanelli.

LOCATION Piazza Fiume, Lido, on the corner of Lungomare Marconi and Via Dalmazia
VAPORETTO Lido–Santa Maria Elisabetta
ACCESS not open to the public

Daniele Calabi 1961–63

CONDOMINIO VILLA MOROSINI

Opening directly on to the water basin opposite the Hotel Excelsior, this development of three apartments extends the design tradition of the 20th-century Venetian Lido villa. Seen from its landward entrance on Via Morosini, it presents solid, understated and precisely detailed façades of white-painted diagonal shutter-boarded concrete panels framing a glazed corner staircase. In complete contrast, its water frontages are a tumbling assembly of open-gridded metal balconies, shutters and blinds. Viewed from the Excelsior, the complexity and bustle of this design is inappropriate to the small scale of the overall building, but when seen from the opposite bank of the canal a balance is restored between the façades. Rising over the whole is an exuberantly detailed communal roof terrace, or *altana*, the traditional Venetian architectural feature.

Other work by the same architect can be seen in a larger residential development at No. 37 Via Dardanelli and its adjacent Via Foscari leading away from the Calabi house in Piazza Fiume. Built in 1987–90, these blocks, clad in coloured metal panels, are reminiscent of the Villa Morosini.

LOCATION Via Francesco Morosini
VAPORETTO Lido–Santa Maria Elisabetta
ACCESS not open to the public

Alessandro Scarpa 1976–79

NEW BLUE MOON BEACH COMPLEX

In *Venezia: La Nuova Architettura*, Giancarlo de Carlo explains how the popular bathing establishment – *Stabilimenti Bagni* – was built on this spot in the middle of the 19th century and was in use until, in 1945, the retreating German army blew it up. Although later reconstructed, the new complex became a conglomeration of cafés and restaurants, without much reference to its previous life. Moreover, the poor post-war building materials soon deteriorated. In the mid 1990s de Carlo was asked to design a more fitting replacement. In doing so, he took account of the history of the Lido and the tenor of the art and literature that it has inspired in its visitors.

There are four elements. First is the two-level pavilion, with a lower covered piazza, an elliptical staircase up to another piazza, open to the sky but sheltered with a cupola. In the middle of the cupola, a spiral staircase rises up like a flagpole. Second, the public gardens that flank the complex are now incorporated in the overall design. Third, there is the beach area, with two walkways, about 6 metres high, with white metal balustrading, that lead sinuously down to the waves on supports above the sand. Behind these is an amphitheatre to be used for concerts, shows and films. Finally, the sweeping wave of the main building is topped with asymmetrical domes. The windows and doors are jade green, giving a period seaside feel to a promising new venue.

LOCATION Piazzale Bucintoro, on the Lungomare Marconi
VAPORETTO Lido–Santa Maria Elisabetta
ACCESS scheduled to open in 2002

Giancarlo de Carlo and associates 1996–2002

THE ARCHITECTS OF VENICE

For much of the period covered by this book, the term 'architect' is somewhat anachronistic. The men who created the great works of Venetian architecture often had a background in stonemasonry and carpentry, and had achieved their design expertise not through formal architectural training, which did not exist *per se*, but on the job – through contact with scholars seeking, for example, to revisit the priniciples of classical Greek and Roman architecture, or through their own study of mathematics, philosophy or art. Sculptors too contributed greatly to the architectural heritage of Venice – their work transforming the façades of churches and enriching the built environment of the city. (Architects not listed here can be found under individual building entries or in the Index.)

BARTOLOMEO BON (c 1410–c 1467) Son of the equally skilful Zane (or Giovanni) Bon, this Venetian-born master-stonemason and sculptor found his *métier* in the highly crafted work of the late-Gothic period. Bon was influenced both by Tuscan and northern architecture. His fine work can be seen, for example, at the Scuola Grande di San Rocco, in the lunette over the Scuola Grande di San Marco entrance, the portal of the Madonna dell'Orto, the west portal of Santi Giovanni e Paolo and the Porta della Carta (Palazzo Ducale). (See also Ca' d'Oro.)

ANTONIO RIZZO (c 1430–99) Originally from Verona, the sculptor Rizzo arrived in Venice around 1460 and was one of the harbingers of the early Renaissance here (see his great Renaissance funerary monument for the Tron family [1476–80] in the Frari). Rizzo quickly won commissions for three altars in San Marco. He also worked at the Palazzo Ducale, both before the 1485 fire – when he sculpted the figures of Adam and Eve for the Arco Foscari in the courtyard, and after it – when he was *proto* (chief surveyor), for the reconstruction of the east wing of the palace. He completed the lower part of the wing and the Scala dei Giganti. (See also Scuola dei Calegheri.)

PIETRO SOLARI (KNOWN AS LOMBARDO) (c 1435–1515) AND FAMILY Born in Carona, Lombardy, Pietro Lombardo ran a successful stonemasons' workshop with two sons, Tullio and Sante. His façades are characterised by applied marble decoration and delicate reliefs – seen in their purest, most complete form in the decoration of the votive church of Santa Maria dei Miracoli. The family was also responsible for the lower orders of the Scuola Grande di San Marco, and Pietro, perhaps most famously, for a series of five monuments to doges (1467–1500) in the church of Santi Giovanni e Paolo. One of these – the tomb of Doge Pasquale Malipiero (early 1470s) was Lombardo's first Venetian work, inspired by the work of Tuscan masters. The more prolific of his sons, Tullio, was also an accomplished sculptor. His *Double Portrait* in the Ca' d'Oro (c 1500) and his relief of the *Coronation of the Virgin* (1500–02) in San Giovanni Crisostomo are particularly fine examples of his work. Sante Lombardo was responsible for San Giorgio dei Greci and worked on the staircase at Scuola Grande di San Rocco. (See also San Giobbe, Palazzo Contarini del Zaffo, Cornaro chapel at Santi Apostoli, Ca' Dario.)

MAURO CODUSSI, SOMETIMES CODUCCI (c 1440–1504) Codussi, born to the north of Venice, moved to the city in 1469. His work – a uniquely Venetian interpretation of Renaissance principles – was a profound influence throughout the so-called transitional period between Gothic and Renaissance. Firstly commissioned to create the church of San Michele in Isola, he went on to complete the church of San Zaccaria and the upper orders of the Scuola Grande di San Marco. His work in palace design was no less assured – see the Palazzo Lando-Corner-Spinelli and the Palazzo Loredan-Vendramin-Calergi (considered his masterpiece). He often worked alongside Pietro Lombardo, and their work is occasionally confused, one with the other. (See also San Giovanni Crisostomo and the campanile of San Pietro in Castello.)

ANTONIO ABBONDI (KNOWN AS SCARPAGNINO) (c 1475–1549) Greatly influenced by Codussi, Scarpagnino's most famous contribution to Venice was the Fabbriche Vecchie – part of a programme that transformed the area round the Rialto. He also designed the staircase for the Scuola Grande di San Rocco and is often credited with the portico to the Fondaco dei Tedeschi. His last work was the church of San Sebastiano with its innovative choir gallery.

MICHELE SANMICHELI (c 1484–1559) Sanmicheli, born in Verona, worked in Rome until its fall in 1527 and moved to Venice full of ideas for a sturdy, robust building style with a Roman influence. He became military architect to the Republic, making a considerable contribution to the fortifications at the Arsenale, and otherwise working abroad for the Republic in Corfu, Crete and Cyprus. His masterpiece in the city, however, was the imposing Palazzo Grimani.

JACOPO SANSOVINO (1486–1570) Like his near contemporary, Sanmicheli, the Florentine Sansovino worked in Rome before fleeing to Venice in 1527. Two years later he was made *proto* for the Procurators of San Marco, and is chiefly responsible for both the form and appearance of today's Piazza San Marco, inspired by the imposing, classical style of Rome (see also Marciana Library). His work in church and palace design was equally influential and much admired by Palladio (see San Francesco della Vigna, San Martino Vescovo, San Zulian, Palazzo Corner della Ca' Grande). Another of his major works was the bronze doors for the sacristy in San Marco. (See also Arsenale, Ca' di Dio, Fabbriche Nuove, San Michele in Isola.)

ANDREA DI PIETRO DELLA GONDOLA (KNOWN AS PALLADIO) (1508–80) A native of Padua, Palladio moved to Vicenza when he was 16 to work as a stonemason, and came under the influence of a great scholar and amateur architect, Giangiorgio Trissino (1478–1550). It was Trissino, a member of the cultural circle of the Medici pope Leo X, who gave Palladio his nickname (after Pallas, Greek god of wisdom), and who introduced his intelligent but uneducated protegé to the principles of classical architecture, through the writings of Sebastiano Serlio and the works of Sanmicheli and Sansovino. By the time he was appointed official architect to the Venetian Republic in 1570 (also the date that his influential *Four Books on Architecture* was published) Palladio had already built his famous country villas for the nobility of Vicenza, had made plans for San Francesco della Vigna and had begun the church of San Giorgio Maggiore.

Palladio was never commissioned to build a private palace on the Grand Canal, and his Roman-inspired five-arched design for the Rialto bridge was turned down in favour of Da Ponte's. But he did revolutionise Venetian church design, and all of Palladio's churches are in Venice. His major innovations were, first, to marry the Renaissance interest in centralised, harmonious spaces with the liturgical demands of monastic foundations (for example, the need for linear processional aisles and choirs separated from the congregation), and secondly, to show that these internal spatial elements could be powerfully reflected on the church façade. Palladio effected this using the model of a classical temple. His work was to inspire much imitation throughout the western world. (See also San Pietro in Castello, Santa Maria della Carità cloisters, San Giorgio Maggiore monastery, Redentore.)

ALESSANDRO VITTORIA (1524–1608) Vittoria was a sculptor rather than an architect, but as such had a considerable influence on the built environment of Venice during the high Renaissance, and was a great influence on the younger generation that followed, for example Girolamo Campagna. His most famous work is probably the early-baroque Palazzo Balbi. (See also San Zulian.)

VINCENZO SCAMOZZI (1552–1616) Before Scamozzi arrived in Venice in 1572, he had already established a reputation in his native Vicenza for designing villas and palaces. He was greatly influenced by Palladio, his buildings incorporating many Palladian features. He travelled widely, producing, among other works, designs for Salzburg Cathedral. In the 1590s, he recorded his design principles in *L'Idea dell'architettura universale* (published 1615). His theories were to have an impact on English neoclassical architecture. In Venice he worked on the Romanised extension for Sansovino's Marciana Library and built the first stage of the Procuratie Nuove. (See also the church of the Tolentini and Rialto Market Buildings.)

BALDASSARE LONGHENA (1598–1682) While most of Venice's most famous architects were not natives of the city, Longhena was Venetian born and bred. He would become a much-respected exponent of a restrained and refined baroque style. Before winning the competition to build his quintessential Venetian masterpiece, the church of Santa Maria della Salute, he had already designed several palaces including the imposing Ca' Rezzonico and Ca' Pesaro. Longhena worked for both the Jewish community in the Ghetto, and the Greek community, for which he designed the complex around the church of San Giorgio dei Greci. The staircase and newly restored library at the San Giorgio Maggiore monastery are his work. (See also Ospedaletto, Scuola Grande dei Carmini.)

GIUSEPPE SARDI (c 1621–99) Along with Longhena, Sardi is considered one of the most important baroque architects, gaining in 1689 the prestigious appointment of *proto* of San Marco – and therefore responsible for the buildings on the Piazza. The extraordinarily ornate but nonetheless fine façade of Santa Maria del Giglio is typical of his church design work. Sardi influenced the next generation of architects, including Antonio Gaspari and Sardi's own nephew, Domenico Rossi. (See also Ospedaletto.)

ANDREA TIRALI (1657–1737) Another Venetian native, son of a builder, and at first a surveyor, Tirali became *proto* of the Magistrato alle Acque, responsible for the maintenance of the Lagoon and sea defences, and then of Piazza when he was responsible for repaving the Piazza and the Piazzetta in 1722–35. Tirali was a contemporary of Domenico Rossi, although unlike Rossi he was more interested in the up and coming neoclassical style than with the baroque. His most effective work in the city is the six-bay neoclassical portico of Scamozzi's Tolentini church and the fine internal staircase at the Palazzo Pisani-Moretta.

DOMENICO ROSSI (1657–1737) Sent to Venice to study architecture under his uncle, Giuseppe Sardi, Rossi was apprenticed as a stonemason in the workshops of Alessandro Tremignon and Baldassare Longhena. Although later disparaged by Tommaso Temanza, who called him 'an uneducated man but well-versed in the practical side of building, who had little or no good taste in art', he was certainly not without talent, and influence, through close connection with the Venetian nobility. In 1709 his baroque design for the façade of the church of San Stae won the competition for its reconstruction. He also collaborated on the design of the Gesuiti.

ANTONIO GASPARI (c 1660–c 1720) A follower of Longhena and a contemporary of Domenico Rossi, Gaspari was responsible for completing Longhena's work at the grand palace of Ca' Pesaro, and also for the Palazzo Zenobio.

GIORGIO MASSARI (1687–1766) Born in Venice, and working there for much of his life (he was made *proto* of San Marco after 1737), Massari also designed villas and churches on the mainland. He was a follower of Tirali, working at the cusp of late baroque and neoclassicism. He completed Longhena's great Palazzo Grassi.

TOMMASO TEMANZA (1705–89) Temanza, a Venetian native, was part of the intellectual and cultural circle of the city, read widely – particularly the architectural treatises of Leon Battista Alberti and Palladio – and enjoyed heated debate about the principles of architecture with his contemporaries. He became a touchstone for a whole generation. He was also interested in town planning, and is credited with work undertaken for the Republic to strengthen the sea defences, to improve the internal watercourses and, effectively, make more permanent the boundaries of Venice. He built the church of the Maddalena (finished after his death by Selva) along neoclassical lines, and was also responsible for constructing a small pavilion in the garden of the Palazzo Zenobio.

GIANNANTONIO SELVA (1753–1819) Selva began his career in Venice during the Republic and ended it under Napoleon. He was a pupil of Temanza and worked closely with his neoclassical master. Chiefly known for his work at the Fenice theatre, Selva also worked on the church of the Maddalena after Temanza's death, and was responsible, with Antonio Diedo, for the church of San Maurizio. Selva went on to execute the Napoleonic proposals for creation of the Via Garibaldi, including the entrance to the Giardini Pubblici.

GIUSEPPE TORRES (1872–1935) Torres, born in Venice, is perhaps best known for his house – the Veneto-Byzantine throw-back, Casa Torres. As a young man he had studied medieval architecture, but his work later developed through the contemporary styles of art nouveau towards the severest minimalism seen at his last great work, the votive temple of Santa Maria della Vittoria, begun in 1918. After the First World War he devoted himself to working with the Opera di Soccorso to reconstruct war-damaged churches. From 1926 to 1935 he was Professor of Sacred Architecture and Monument Restoration at the Venice School of Architecture. After his death, his place at the university was filled by his assistant, Angelo Scattolin, architect of the Cassa di Risparmio and the extension to the Palazzo del Cinema.

CARLO SCARPA (1906–78) In his lifetime often dismissed as 'an artist who wanted to build', Scarpa can now been seen as one of the foremost 20th-century Italian architects. Respected particularly for his ability to combine innovative design with a sensitive understanding of traditional craftsmanship and materials, his work captures the spirit of its specific location and thus continues the great tradition of Venetian architects in their creation of uniquely Venetian works. Chiefly feted for his museum projects, such as his work at the

THE ARCHITECTS OF VENICE

VENICE: AN ARCHITECTURAL GUIDE

museum of the Castelvecchio in Verona, he worked extensively, with his assistant Sergio Los, in Venice. Examples include the remodelling of the Palazzo Querini Stampalia, the Olivetti showroom, internal galleries of the Ca' d'Oro, the School of Architecture entrance at the Tolentini and the water's-edge Monumento alla Partigiana.

GIANCARLO DE CARLO (BORN 1919) De Carlo, a native of Genoa, lives and works in Milan, but is also a professor at the Venice School of Architecture and at the University Faculty of Architecture in Genoa. His work, often in the sensitive remodelling and extension of historic buildings, has attracted much acclaim, winning several prestigious awards in the international architectural community. In Venice, his new residential housing on the island of Mazzorbo , currently being extended, has been a successful architectural and community project. (See also the New Blue Moon complex on the Lido.)

GINO VALLE (BORN 1923) Originally from Udine in the Veneto, Valle studied at the University of Venice School of Architecture and at Harvard. Early in his career he worked with Carlo Scarpa and Giuseppe Samonà, and in 1948 he joined his father's studio in Udine. In 1987 he returned to Venice to teach at his old university, where he is currently a professor. His reputation is international, and his works are to be found in New York, Berlin and Vienna as well as in Italy. He is also a painter and designer. He was responsible for the much acclaimed IACP Complex, a modern residential housing complex on the Giudecca with many references to traditional Venetian architectural features.

VITTORIO GREGOTTI (BORN 1927) Gregotti, whose public housing at San Giobbe seeks to create a modern version of the traditional Venetian residential cityscape, was born in Novara, and graduated from Milan Polytechnic. He established his own company, Gregotti Associati, in 1974 and is currently Professor of Architectural Composition at the Venice School of Architecture.

VALERIANO PASTOR (BORN 1927) Pastor was born in Trieste and now lives and works in Venice. He has taught at the Venice School of Architecture since 1977, where he is currently Professor of Urban Design. Much of his work has been in Venice and the nearby mainland. From 1983 to 1997 he was involved in the remodeling of the Palazzo Querini Stampalia, and from 1989 to 1999 in restoration at Ca' Foscari University. In housing, his work can be seen on Giudecca in a residential complex (1982–89) at Sacca Fisola facing Gino Valle's IACP Complex across the Canale dei Lavraneri, and at the ex-Ice Factory.

CINO ZUCCHI (BORN 1955) Based in Milan, where he is a professor of design, Zucchi's current work at the ex-Junghans Factory is revitalising an area of run-down post-industrial Venice. Other works include the Porta Serrata at Ravenna and his prize-winning (Europan 3) proposals for the Piazza Sofia in Turin.

INDEX

INDEX

INDEX

Photographs are by Keith Collie,
    except:
pages 3.45, 4.9, 4.13, 4.19, 4.21,
    4.36, 5.21, 5.29, 5.39, 5.54,
    6.11, 8.2, 9.11 Simon Pilling
page 2.39 Corbis
page 5.41 Christopher Tadgell

NORWAY
A GUIDE TO RECENT ARCHITECTURE

Ingerid Helsing Almaas

Recent Norwegian architecture has been dominated by the themes of infrastructure and travel, connecting the country's regions and offsetting the domination of Oslo and the ubiquity of single-family houses in a country where anyone with a little spare money can build their dream home. Around 100 projects built during the last fifteen years have been chosen to represent an architectural tradition of great quality and innovation, predominantly the work of young architects working within a context of prosperity and plentiful land.

0 7134 8782 8/£12.99

THE GOOD PLACE GUIDE
URBAN DESIGN IN BRITAIN AND IRELAND

John Billingham and Richard Cole

The Good Place Guide describes more than 120 places throughout Great Britain and Ireland that people will enjoy using or visiting. It concentrates on places that have been created or significantly changed over the last 50 years and that are good examples of the design of places as distinct from individual buildings. It will be eye-opening both for people professionally concerned with the design of urban spaces and for the rest of us who have to use them.

0 7134 8786 0/£12.99